Changing Your Story

Changing Your Story

20 Life Lessons Drawn from Elite Sport

BILL BESWICK

PENGUIN LIFE

AN IMPRINT OF

PENGUIN BOOKS

PENGUIN LIFE

UK | USA | Canada | Ireland | Australia
India | New Zealand | South Africa

Penguin Life is part of the Penguin Random House group of companies
whose addresses can be found at global.penguinrandomhouse.com.

First published 2021
001

Copyright © Bill Beswick, 2021

The moral right of the author has been asserted

Set in 13.5/16 pt Garamond MT Std
Typeset by Jouve (UK), Milton Keynes
Printed and bound in Great Britain by Clays Ltd, Elcograf S.p.A.

The authorized representative in the EEA is Penguin Random House Ireland,
Morrison Chambers, 32 Nassau Street, Dublin D02 YH68

A CIP catalogue record for this book is available from the British Library

ISBN: 978–0–241–44801–4

www.greenpenguin.co.uk

To my much-loved grandchildren, Tom, Lucy, Katy, Alfie, Arlo and Otis. I trust you all to change the story for our family in new and wonderful ways.

Contents

CONTENTS

Foreword

It has been my good fortune to naturally have a strong competitive mindset, and that has been reinforced during my time as a swimmer for Great Britain with the introduction of sport psychology and Bill Beswick. Bill shared with us new perspectives to high performance and the first thing he said has always stuck in my mind: 'the mind is the athlete, the body simply the means.'

From that moment on my coach, Mel Marshall, and I have made the training of my mind an important part of our preparation. I've worked constantly to become a champion and that is in large part due to my thinking like a champion every day at training. There have been problems of course and a couple of setbacks, but Bill taught us to deal with, and not react to, such difficulties.

It is great that in this book you can share the stories that I enjoyed and learned from, plus some of the strategies for building mental strength and keeping emotional control – key arena skills – that played a significant part in Great Britain's swimming success in the 2016 Olympic Games. On one evening in Rio in front of a capacity crowd and the world's television audience I had just fifty-seven seconds to produce the performance of my life and win the gold medal. At that moment the mind takes over and tests your ability to produce a disciplined performance under pressure. Superb physical preparation and a focused and strong mindset were the keys to my success.

It is my belief that the experience of high-performance swimming and its physical and mental challenges have made me a better person as well as athlete. In this book Bill offers you an opportunity to grow your mind and think like a champion. I recommend it to you!

Adam Peaty MBE
World, Olympic, European,
Commonwealth and British Champion

Introduction

This is a book of stories. I was raised to be a storyteller. On Sundays in a house without television my father would ask each of his four sons (I was the youngest) to tell the story of their football or rugby game the previous day. The king of storytellers was my eldest brother, Fred, and each week the way he brought his game to life stayed with me for many days. His team was heroic, the opponents were the villains, and the plot was always overcoming the threat of failure to gain an improbable victory. Fred, often the hero, was fortunate that his stories were told in the days before cameras recorded the truth! These were fascinating stories for a young boy, and I used them to imagine what I would have done in the same circumstances. It was no surprise that sport became my main interest and storytelling became part of my style as a teacher, coach, lecturer and performance psychologist.

Years later, I was to encounter another fireside storyteller, who reminded me that stories are not just central to who we are as individuals but the glue that holds us to other people. Before the fall of the Iron Curtain, I was one of a group of college lecturers visiting the then

Czechoslovakia to promote higher education. One evening, I was invited by our host liaison officer to a barbecue at the edge of a small town. It was a simple bonfire in the middle of a field with sausages and potatoes cooked on the fire. Drinks were very limited. The highlight of the evening was when an old man suddenly got up from his seat and began walking around the fire. Everybody joined him apart from me. I stayed watching, absorbed by what was happening. My host explained that this was the village storyteller who maintained and retold the myths and legends of their shared history, reinforcing their community heritage and adding stories of the recent past. As I saw how engaged, energized and connected the crowd was with the storyteller, the power of storytelling was underlined in a unique yet universal way.

Humans are storytelling creatures, and the importance of storytelling is well documented by anthropologists and social scientists. Although the means of communication has evolved from cave paintings to today's social media, the influence of powerful stories has not lessened. Culture is absorbed, and life lessons can be learned through the heritage of stories passed from one generation to the next, across communities and through interest and friendship groups. Stories emotionalize information, validate behaviour and forge social connections, and that makes them memorable as a basis for changing our lives.

The world of sport is perfect for stories, because sport is not just motion but 'motion wrapped in emotion'. It is full of unlikely heroes, love-to-hate bad guys, the triumphs of the underdog and against-all-odds victories. From my brother's fireside tall tales to the most dramatic and exciting Olympic and World Cup victories (or defeats!) the stories we tell from the sporting world have a way of capturing our imaginations and inspiring our actions outside of the arena. Life and sport are both about human connection, and stories, with their emotional power to convey messages with impact, connect us to the lives of others. Stories are particularly powerful when they carry meaning that helps us make sense of our own lives.

Nobody understood the power of stories and emotion to help people face their challenges better than the late, great USA basketball coach Jim Valvano. Jim was a wonderful storyteller who was diagnosed with terminal cancer at the age of forty-six. He was persuaded to make one final speech. Helped onto the stage, his last message was:

> We should do three things every day of our life. Number one is laugh. You should laugh every day. Number two is to think, we should spend some time in thought. And, number three is you should have your emotions moved to tears. If you laugh, think and cry, that is one heck of a day.

Jim understood that life can be both joy and pain, and that it's OK to be imperfect and vulnerable providing you accept and embrace it.

Stories from sport are particularly valuable because, though sport is seen primarily as physical activity, a challenging contest can arouse a range of emotions and reactions and thus reflect many of the situations we meet in our ordinary lives. The athlete's emotional intelligence and ability to control themselves will determine whether these emotions are empowering or disempowering. In addition, sport is seen as individual and highly competitive, though it is, in fact, remarkably social and collaborative. In sport we see 'ordinary people doing extraordinary things' (taken from another Jim Valvano quote). I have come to regard sport as stories of human connection under challenge, competition, pressure and fatigue, dominated by the intangibles of thoughts and feelings.

There are those people in sport who believe if you can't measure it, it isn't worthwhile. (I have heard of a sign in the sports science office of a Premier League football club that reads, 'If you can't measure it, it doesn't exist'.) I don't agree. Most human endeavours, sport included, involve a mix of physical and mental efforts. The measurable components, for example, lung capacity, are important in performance but so too are the non-measurable, mental aspects, such as belief.

The key transformational moment in my long career in sport – playing, teaching, coaching and supporting performance – was when I finally understood that the mind was the athlete and the body simply the means.

How you think, and therefore feel, is vital in releasing positive energy and realizing your physical abilities to the full. Sport teaches you to understand yourself better and come to terms with the strength of character needed to face challenges and how to learn to overcome failures. In the end it's not about what you achieve but who you become. The stories I tell in the pages of this book give insights into experiences such as decision-making, overcoming fear, feelings of worthlessness and vulnerability, and led to many instances of great success both in sport and elsewhere in life.

Everybody wants to be a top performer in their life, not just those involved in sport. However, what often happens is that the treadmill of life's daily challenges wears down our good intentions and we accept a lesser life. Stephen Grosz, the psychoanalyst, puts it this way: 'At one time or another most of us have felt trapped by things we find ourselves thinking or doing, caught by our own impulses or foolish choices, ensnared on some unhappiness or fear, imprisoned by our own history.' Because my work is about changing thinking and behaviour, taking people from negative to positive, this book contains many lessons to help readers become mentally and emotionally stronger. The reason that athletes succeed is that they, as distinct from the general population, are taught the physical and mental strategies of building and maintaining high performance. My experiences allow you moments inside the arena with the elite athletes and would-be champions with whom I have worked. This gives you the opportunity to share the strategies and tactics that have helped athletes and their coaches overcome their stress and anxiety and meet challenges. I hope these processes are presented in ways that encourage you to adopt them in your own search for a more fulfilling life.

This book tells stories drawn from my personal and sporting life, spanning grass-roots recreation through student and representative competition to professional and international level in this country, Europe and the USA. I share experiences from years as a coach, with a Commonwealth gold medal for basketball and an English Football League Cup winners' medal on the study shelf and as a performance psychologist with clubs such as Manchester United, Derby County and Middlesbrough, as well as supporting England or Great Britain teams of both genders in football, rugby, basketball and swimming. Although many of the athletes featured in the stories were happy for me to use their names, in the spirit of confidentiality, and helping readers concentrate on the message of the story, I decided on anonymity. However, role models, with stories in the public domain, have been identified.

I present my stories to audiences in sport, education and business. While most people find them interesting and entertaining, there are some who are left deeply affected and influenced by them. I have continued to mentor (or act as a 'thinking partner' for) those who are determined to make changes in their life, and it has been one of my greatest pleasures advising, encouraging and stretching them to meet their goals. All of us have moments of helplessness and vulnerability, when we need someone to help us find a new direction and harness new energy. The stories have also helped give my own life meaning and purpose, and my hope is that, though I cannot directly mentor you, sharing them helps you take control of your life story and own it rather than letting it own you.

The first step is to accept responsibility for controlling your own destiny. There is no age limit to this. You can take yourself in a fresh direction at any point in your life providing you maintain a strong and resilient mindset. When the film star Clint Eastwood was playing golf the following conversation was recorded:

Partner: 'How old are you, Clint?'
Clint: 'I turn eighty-eight on Monday.'
Partner: 'What are you going to do?'
Clint: 'I am going to start a new movie.'
Partner: 'What keeps you going?'
Clint: 'I get up every day and don't let the old man in.'

That story has had a powerful impact on me. I have Parkinson's disease (PD), and though age and this disorder shapes physical condition, as with Clint, it need not stop you developing a mindset to achieve. The choice between fighter and victim is always yours. I may have PD – but it does not have me! You become what you think!

Let's give the final word in this introduction to Aleksandr Solzhenitsyn, the Russian author whose life was a constant challenge. He said: 'If you want to change the world, who do you begin with, yourself or others? I believe if we begin with ourselves and do the things we need to do and become the best person we can be, we have a much better chance of changing the world for the better.'

'TAKE CONTROL OF YOUR STORY AND OWN IT RATHER THAN LETTING IT OWN YOU'

LESSON 1:

TAKE RESPONSIBILITY – CROSS THE LINE

I was regarded as a pioneer of sport psychology when I started work at Derby County FC in 1995. There was very little understanding then about how psychology could work in a football club. There was no curriculum for me to refer to, so I flew by the seat of my pants – necessity breeding creativity.

One thing I did know from study trips to the USA was that I should see players one on one and help them deal with their performance issues. American sport psychologists recognized that mental and emotional barriers could severely limit performance and that players would only reveal such perceived weaknesses in a confidential one-to-one environment. Reviewing my notes from initial sessions with the club players showed a consistent pattern emerged. Players were blaming others or making excuses for their performance failures. Time after time, I noted down that – in my view – the player was not taking responsibility for his situation.

When the team returned from their first break of the season, I asked the manager, Jim Smith, whether I could talk to them. Jim agreed, and when the team gathered I told them the story of my background in Manchester. I was the youngest child of a family living in constrained circumstances with limited expectations for us children. However, passing for grammar school gave me a different view on life. My father, a semi-skilled labourer of limited education but smart, recognized this and gave me a rare piece of advice.

He drew a line across the floor and told me that the line represented an important choice in life. Staying this side of the line, which circumstances had forced him to do, meant living a life where others told you what to do and you simply accepted your fate. This was not what he expected of me. He urged me to cross the line and be the one who defined my own life. However, taking this step would mean taking responsibility for my situation, plus accepting that there would be the occasional failure.

I shared with the players the realization that my father was referring to one of my brothers who reacted badly to any failure, becoming overwhelmed because he took it personally and emotionally. Unfortunately, my brother compensated for this loss of mental and emotional stability by turning to alcohol, and what was a minor issue became a major problem.

I told the players that the reason I was standing in front of them, sharing these experiences, was that throughout my life I have always crossed the line. Even when excuses were plentiful and blaming others would be easier, I still took responsibility. I had learned that although sometimes you cannot choose the situation you find yourself in (bad things do happen in life), you can always choose your response.

Judging the situation carefully, I then told the players what a difference it could make to their lives and careers if they could find the courage to take responsibility for the situations in which they found themselves. I reminded them that maturity is defined as taking responsibility for the control and direction of one's life. To guide their future actions, I provided the simple definition that the great NFL coach Bill Belichick gives his players:

> Responsibility means doing what you're supposed to do, when you're supposed to do it. It means being where you're supposed to be, when you're supposed to be there. It means doing what you say you're going to do, and doing right by yourself and by others.

This talk made a distinct impression on the players. A number of them showed a significant improvement in their ability to deal with the issues that had limited their performance, such as lack of timekeeping, focus and attention in training and general poor work ethic. For one player in particular, the talk proved to be a turning point. George was talented but had refused to change his poor lifestyle, despite his coaches warning that this would eventually undermine his progress. Slowly George learned to take back control of his life. The coaches and I could see how he began to avoid attractive but ultimately bad decisions, made better friendship choices, created much better lifestyle patterns, learned not to make commitments that he would regret and generally walked taller because he was earning the trust of his teammates and coaches.

Self-discipline is not easy and asks people to move from the comfortable – avoiding responsibility and blaming others – to the uncomfortable – taking responsibility and accepting accountability. I like the way Susan David expresses this need in her book *Emotional Agility*:

> As with every hero's journey, our movement to a better life begins with showing up. But that doesn't mean we have to smile or slay all the demons. It does mean we must face up to, make peace with, and find an honest and open way to live with them. When we show up fully even the worst demons usually back down.

The first line you have to cross is to show up and face the challenges that your environment poses. For most of us, these include holding down a responsible job, building positive relationships and meeting our financial commitments. You can only achieve these and flourish if you learn to control your emotions and stay positive, avoid the excuses to do nothing and stay resilient in the face of difficulties.

Having now practised performance psychology for

'HAVE THE COURAGE TO CROSS THE LINE'

over thirty years, I fully appreciate the importance of that initial lesson. The first step for a fully functioning athlete or adult is to take responsibility and accountability for your situation and the actions you take. This acts as the foundation for building the mental strength necessary to deal with the challenges of sport and life. It is, of course, always easier to blame others or find excuses. However, if you have the courage to cross the line, you have the rewards of a fuller, more successful and satisfying life.

PUT IT INTO ACTION

- Train yourself to face a new challenge with the immediate response, 'how can I best deal with this?'
- Stop making excuses or blaming. Notice when you naturally do this and think how you can take responsibility.

LESSON 2:

FIND YOUR REASON WHY – AND CHOOSE AN 'A' GRADE LIFE

Early in my career as a performance psychologist, I met one of the most exceptional football players I have worked with. Darren was perhaps not the most talented athlete physically but so strong mentally he could best be described as a warrior-athlete. This made him especially interesting to work with. Darren challenged everybody every day to be better and did not suffer fools, or the lazy, gladly. I was impressed with his standards and performance in both training and games. However, when I told him so, he was totally unaffected and ignored me. I was at a loss as to how to understand him or how to build a relationship with him. The answer came from a comment from the club's kit man, who said that Darren could only function when challenged. The next day, I mentioned to Darren an aspect of his performance that he could improve. He became engaged, and as we explored the topic, I finally realized that the strong desire for continual improvement was what made Darren different.

This was his reason 'why' – the motivation that created his extraordinary passion and commitment. He pushed himself to the limits every day to enjoy the feeling of improving. He only became irritated, short-tempered and difficult to coach when this was not happening. This self-imposed pressure characterizes high-performers: it is the ability to apply discipline, focus and energy day after day despite fatigue and external stresses in order to become the athlete they want to be.

So I was not surprised that Darren particularly loved the story of a group of molecular biology students at college in the USA who were intending to go on to medical training. As the students reached the end of their course, they only had to complete a final examination. Before the examination, the professor gave them a surprise. In recognition of their outstanding work during the course, he was in a position to award them an automatic B grade. Not only had they passed the course, they need not take the examination.

As you can imagine there was a sigh of relief, and all but one of the students leaped to their feet and headed, presumably, for the nearest bar. The professor repeated his offer to the lone student sat in the hall. He remained seated and awaited the examination paper. The final exam consisted of two sentences. 'Congratulations,' it read, 'you have received an A in this class. Keep believing in yourself.' It was a just reward for the student with a powerful reason 'why' (to be the best he could), who had worked hard and believed in himself.

When beginning discussions with high-performance

athletes, I tell them that the best I can do is share ideas. I cannot programme their behaviour because they alone choose their actions and they alone are responsible for their behaviour. All control is firmly placed in the hands of each athlete, and all I can do is share some ideas on what might be the best decisions they could make in particular circumstances. Taking responsibility can be challenging, but it is the key to developing consistent high-performance behaviour.

Both Darren and the biology student had a remarkable passion to achieve the highest of standards. To make an important change in your situation, the important thing is to establish clarity of passion and purpose – the reason *why* you want to change and where you want to get. To do this I always start my mentoring support by asking a client three key questions:

- What do you want?
- How badly do you want it?
- How much are you willing to suffer?

The answers to these questions form the foundation for a behavioural drive to change and improve. A key part of my work is to help clients connect their reason why – what they want to achieve – with their how – the plan to make that happen. When these questions were posed to a team that had won all its competitions the season before, a ready-made excuse to relax a little, the answers were a clear example of the power of the reason why. They collectively replied that they wanted to:

- win again;
- win better;
- win with class.

I tell the athletes sat in front of me that they make choices every day that determine the grade of life they lead. I ask them to describe the differences between an A grade, a B grade and a C grade athlete or person. The difference usually centres on the level of commitment to maximize on the resources at their disposal and to take full advantage of the opportunities before them – that is a choice that everybody, not just athletes, makes every day. However, increasing your level of commitment is uncomfortable, it demands more time and effort. Most people settle for the comfort of a lesser-grade life. I then ask the athletes to picture themselves as an A grade athlete and to describe the story of their career. Wonderful stories emerge of how they make the best of their unique potential and achieve great success. Everybody should want to and can lead an A grade life but like the extraordinary student they have to commit to making the difficult A grade choice every day.

There are, of course, a thousand excuses not to take the time and effort needed to commit to an A Grade choice. However, probably not a single reason not to try.

'YOUR LIFE IS YOUR CHOICE – FIND YOUR WHY!'

In order to succeed you need to find a reason why that generates the passion and commitment to enable you to choose the life you want to lead. Your life is your choice – find your why!

PUT IT INTO ACTION

Define what is important to you in life – and set goals that take you there:

- What do you want to accomplish?
- What kind of impact do you want to have?
- How do you want to be remembered?

LESSON 3:

CHANGE YOUR STORY – LEARN TO BE A WINNER

Some years ago, I received a phone call at my Cheshire home office from James, a top American college soccer coach. He explained to me that he had found himself in a perfect storm and was in real trouble. In two days' time, his team was due to play the number-one college team in the nation. They were playing at home and, for the first time, all the tickets were sold, plus they were the feature game on a national television channel. His problem was that the team was missing five regular players through injury and that very day had four more players suspended with issues over drugs. This meant that he would have to start the game with at least five eighteen-year-old freshmen, three of whom had not yet played for the first team. He sounded desperate and defeated and asked for help. To his surprise, I told him that I was going to put the phone down and wanted him to call me back in an hour. I added that I didn't like the story and needed him to change the story he was telling. Then I ended the call.

One hour later, James rang back and in a very excited

voice told me that his team had a wonderful opportunity coming up in two days' time. They would play the number-one-ranked college team with full national TV coverage – an exciting challenge – and would be playing at home in front of a full, enthusiastic and supportive crowd. Not only that, he would be able to show his coaching skill in demonstrating that his young team could win a game against all the odds by organization, enthusiasm and energy. I commended Coach James on the new story and asked him to let me know the result. Two days later (in the middle of the night, of course), a text arrived: 'Won 2:0 – thank you.'

Everyone has found themselves panicking like James when an important event is coming up and everything seems to be going wrong. I once heard Ellen MacArthur, the youngest person to sail around the world single-handed, reveal in a speech how she was able to deal with the mast breaking but cried for a day when she ran out of teabags. It is also the pitter-patter of multiple little things going wrong that can unnerve us.

The best thing James did was to share the problem and his feelings with someone he trusted. I am totally aware that when meeting a client as a trusted and impartial adviser I may be the only person with whom they feel able to share their fears and anxieties. Although together we may not find a ready solution to their issues, they often tell me how much better they feel after the session. As my mother would often say, 'a problem shared is a problem halved'. Everybody should seek a 'neutral friend' that they can share with, so I was pleased James came to me.

Busy people often are caught in what I call a 'treadmill mindset', too busy to think. How often I have started the season with a coach who wanted to discuss philosophy and strategy only to find a couple of months into the season that they could only focus on how to get through the day. The pressures of modern life, the demand to compete and achieve or simply just to keep up place all of us on the treadmill at some stage. A popular saying in sport, often attributed to the late, great American football coach Vince Lombardi, is that 'fatigue makes cowards of us all'. The treadmill, in the gym and in life, is a conveyor belt that demands constant movement and is draining both of energy and of emotion. How often has any one of us been in that state and later regretted our actions? There was a time when I was able to ride the treadmill of work though would come home tired and emotionally off-balance with very little to offer the most important relationships of my life (apologies to my wife and sons here!).

The one-hour space was enough for Coach James to get off the treadmill and into a 'mental time-out' where he could get beyond his emotions, fear, uncertainty and the dread of being embarrassed, and return to his usual thinking mode. Only then could he get to grips with his challenge and begin to see a bigger picture. As he slowly moved back into a positive state of mind, James began to see opportunities, not problems. Very often, our first interpretation of a situation is to perceive it as a problem, distorted by negative emotions. Like James, it is important to learn the mental discipline of 'parking' the initial response and reframing the interpretation more rationally. When this happens, positivity and energy return, and we can see ways forward. This is the way to turn what is initially seen as a problem into an opportunity.

Rather than waste time and energy worrying about uncontrollables, James was now firmly locked into a solution focus. By the time he had made the second call, James was back in his usual 'fighter mentality' – energetic, taking responsibility, in control and enjoying the challenge. He had left behind his initial 'victim mentality' – passive, finding excuses easy and looking to hide under the pressure. His new body language, speech and enthusiasm had an energizing effect on the young team he was responsible for leading.

My role as a thinking partner to those facing challenges is to allow them the space to get off the treadmill, get beyond their emotions and up into a 'helicopter' to see the big picture with all its opportunities. We will all face similar situations to James in meeting the challenges of life and will have the same choice – victim or fighter. James's dramatic change of mindset offers a valuable strategy that is, with attention and discipline, simple to adopt. If you don't like your story, you too can change it!

'IF YOU DON'T LIKE YOUR STORY, YOU TOO CAN CHANGE IT!'

Note: Two years later James received the National Soccer Coaches Association of America award as the top college soccer coach in the country. My wife and I were there to see him receive it.

PUT IT INTO ACTION

- Next time you feel overwhelmed or out of control of the situation you find yourself in, take a 'time-out' and reframe your narrative to write yourself as the winner.
- Find yourself a 'thinking partner'.
- You are the author of your own story, how do you want to tell it?

LESSON 4:

SET NO LIMITS – BELIEVE IN YOURSELF

Harry's mother gave me the clue as to what was limiting her son's performance. Harry, a tall, powerful and talented fifteen-year-old tennis player, had begun to see me because he was underperforming at big events. Harry's mother disclosed that her son had won his first two matches at the Wimbledon junior tournament in good style, and they were feeling very positive about his chances of reaching the semi-final stage of the tournament. However, on the way to his third match, Harry had overheard his coach explaining to another coach that their next opponent ranked thirty places above him. This clearly had a negative effect on Harry, who suddenly performed badly in the match later that day.

Harry confessed that the information on ranking put him in awe of his opponent. In his mind, he had already anticipated the result and so performed accordingly. This was a clear example of a self-fulfilling prophecy, where behaviour follows expectations and we become what we think. Harry had completely lost sight of his accomplishments in the previous two matches and, believing that his opponent was better than him because of the rankings, had 'choked'. In essence, he beat himself before he even set foot on the court. In my experience, this is a common reaction when young athletes are still developing self-belief.

Environment, upbringing and the significant people in your life all contribute to the picture you have of yourself. How you see yourself creates your reality, and your expectations for yourself become your behavioural norms. Mahatma Gandhi said, 'Your beliefs become your thoughts, your thoughts become your words, your words become your actions, your actions become your habits, your habits become your values, your values become your destiny.' One football coach instinctively modelled his style and behaviour on his father, a former coach whom he had observed throughout his growing-up. This was his image of how coaches should act. It took time to break his self-imposed limits and persuade him that he could be different and better, with a style more effective for his generation.

Our beliefs and thinking patterns have been shaped by the emotional blueprints of our childhood plus other significant experiences and can create the inner obstacles that can make it difficult for us to believe in ourselves or even see ourselves clearly, so even the slightest mishap can send us into negative self-talk. Like Harry we become distracted by our own thought processes, think about everything that can go wrong, focus on what

'HOW YOU
SEE YOURSELF
CREATES YOUR
REALITY'

everybody else is doing and stop trusting ourselves. We beat ourselves up. A simple self-identity check for children is to ask them to draw a picture with themselves in it. A friend of mine with two boys saw one draw himself in the corner of the page while the other drew himself in the centre of his picture. This exactly matched their approach to life: one seized life's opportunities, and the other lived on the periphery.

In the early part of my life, I actually identified with this suffering and believed I was only acting out my destiny. Almost instinctively I held back and operated on the 'edge of the picture' and had to wait until the more positive forces in my life – academic, career and sporting success, together with marriage and raising a family – gathered enough of a critical mass to allow me to remove the limits I had set on myself.

I often explain the power of setting a positive picture of yourself by telling this story of the three bricklayers. A man passing by a building site stopped and asked a bricklayer what he was doing. 'I'm laying bricks,' he replied. When a second bricklayer was asked the same question, he answered he was earning £10 an hour. However, when it came to the third worker, his reply was that he was building a cathedral and would be proud to show his grandchildren what he had helped to create. They were all doing the same task but they saw their role in it completely differently, and that had a big impact on their approach to their job.

If we can find real meaning in the tasks we do, it will elevate the quality and success of the outcomes, and we will be creating a better version of ourselves.

Identifying what was blocking Harry from success, we agreed a four-step programme to stretch his self-imposed limits. First of all, Harry wrote out a history of his achievements to this point in life. As Harry listed off the countless wins in his young career, it was very clear there was no evidence to support his doubts and fears that he was not good enough to take on his opponent. Secondly, we worked together on what I call a 'picture of perfection'. This is a vision of the very best that could happen, assuming all goes well. Harry saw himself in the centre of the picture, playing strong and assertive tennis, winning a major tournament, collecting the trophy and celebrating with his coach and family. This vision excited Harry and reignited his passion. Next, I encouraged Harry to find a 'belief partner', a family member or close friend who constantly urges you onwards and upwards to better things. Harry picked his mother, who was with him at every tournament and was there as his number-one cheerleader whenever the self-doubt and negative self-talk crept in.

Finally, Harry's fourth action was to build achievement momentum by always asking, 'What's next?' I told him and his mother about Adam Peaty, the champion swimmer. Minutes after Adam had won his first European title he was interviewed at the poolside. Asked what he was thinking, Adam replied, 'What's next?' Later in his career, after he had won Olympic gold for the 100 metres breaststroke in 57.1 seconds, Adam immediately announced that next would be Project 56 – his aim to be the first swimmer ever to swim the 100 metres breaststroke in 56 seconds. Adam achieved this two years later, demonstrating the power of a 'What's next?' mentality.

Harry attacked his four-point programme with enthusiasm, putting aside his previous self-imposed limits. Slowly a new Harry is emerging with performances beginning to demonstrate increased toughness and ambition. At the same time, there is still a need for patience while he physically and emotionally matures.

PUT IT INTO ACTION

- Don't set limits on yourself – there is always much more you can achieve.
- Make a list of your personal successes, big or small.
- Create your 'Picture of Perfection' – what's the best that could happen?
- Find a belief partner – someone close who believes in you and motivates you to be better.
- Develop a 'What's next?' attitude to build achievement momentum.

LESSON 5:

PERFORMANCE FOLLOWS ATTITUDE – HAVE YOU CHECKED YOUR ATTITUDE TODAY?

I am often asked who are the most remarkable athletes I have worked with in my long career. As well as listing the footballers Roy Keane, Jamie Carragher and Steven Gerrard (plus Darren, whose story opens Lesson 2), rugby players Owen Farrell and Ben Youngs, plus Olympic swimmer Adam Peaty, I also mention Yasmin, a young teenager from Liverpool. She was especially proud to be captain of her school football team. When I first heard about Yasmin it was because her team had reached the final of the Liverpool Schools Cup that was to be played at Anfield, home of Liverpool Football Club. As all the school finals were being played on the same day, the crowd was much bigger than the girls had ever faced. Although her team were extremely nervous, Yasmin drove them to a 1–1 score at full-time.

The game was tied, so the referee called both captains across and, acknowledging their fatigue, offered them the choice of sharing the trophy for six months each or playing extra time. Both captains consulted with their teams. Yasmin's team was adamant that they had had enough and would settle for sharing. When the two captains reported back, the other captain said they would share, but Yasmin requested extra time. Yasmin went back to her team and told them that the opposition wanted extra time. At the end of extra time the score was still 1–1, and the referee repeated the offer to both captains: this time to share the trophy or face a penalty shootout. Once more, Yasmin's team voted to share, especially the goalkeeper, who couldn't face such responsibility in front of a large crowd. Again, the opposition captain asked to share the trophy and – you guessed it – Yasmin declined, saying her team wanted a penalty shootout. After reporting back to her team that the other captain had requested a penalty shootout, Yasmin elected to take the first penalty. After scoring she did not celebrate but ran immediately to her goalkeeper and took the jersey from her. Yasmin saved three of the penalties, and the game was finally won. When asked by the local media why she had gone to such lengths to win, she replied, 'I dream about football all the time but I only dream of winning, never sharing.' What made this story more remarkable was that when the teacher in charge of the opposition paid tribute to Yasmin as a remarkable young leader, he also mentioned that this was surprising, as she was probably one of the players with the least technical ability on the field.

When I asked a group of young students at my local high school what Yasmin could teach them, one bright girl replied, 'Don't use lack of talent as an excuse. Get your attitude right and give the best performance you are capable of.' The cornerstones of performance are talent and attitude. Excellent performance is almost guaranteed for the person with excellent talent and excellent attitude. However, successful performance varies, often disappointingly, for the person with good talent but poor attitude. One of the pleasures of my career has been encouraging those people like Yasmin, with limited talent but incredible attitude. Jamie Carragher rated himself B on talent – not quite big enough or fast enough or skilled enough. However, he scored A-plus for attitude and, driven by that power, played over five hundred games for Liverpool and more than fifty for England.

You can often succeed with limited talent but never with limited attitude. Performance begins in the head, and successful people think differently from unsuccessful people. Once your attitude is right, good performance is much more likely to follow, and the good news is that though improving your talent can be difficult and take time, you can boost your attitude significantly any time you choose.

High performance in any field inevitably means leaving your comfort zone and facing up to high expectations, stress, some failures, overload, uncertainty and probably some pressure on your relationships. Talent alone cannot resolve these. It is your positive attitude that will provide the mental strength to overcome them. Most of the athletes on my remarkable list combined high talent and great attitude, except Yasmin. That young woman, like Jamie Carragher, maximized ability with the sheer force of passion and persistence.

Early in one season, I had an emergency phone call from Chris, a very talented professional football player, who had reached a personal crisis point. When we met, he bemoaned his circumstances: he had been injured, he was out of the team, the coach did not like him, the media were criticizing him, and so on. Here was a very clear example of the link between attitude and performance. As Chris began to experience some performance problems and a resulting loss of confidence, his attitude declined into a negative cycle where issues were magnified out of proportion. Further discussions confirmed he was in denial:

- covering up for mistakes;
- avoiding talking to the coaches;
- looking for somebody to blame;
- not trying as hard as he could;
- not facing the facts;
- setting unrealistic goals.

A key part of my role can be to act as the 'truth-teller', and what Chris needed at this time was some straight talk, clearing the way for him to change his attitude and take responsibility for his situation. We began by moving

'PERFORMANCE FOLLOWS ATTITUDE'

Chris from his limited personal view to a bigger picture that acknowledged that he had not suddenly become a bad player but was a good player going through a bad time. He admitted that he had not been putting as much effort and focus into practice as usual, needed to step this up and would achieve some small goals even if his big goal – getting back in the first team – eluded him. Finally, Chris accepted that his negative self-talk was hurting him and he must be more positive about his ability to control his circumstances.

He had been focusing on things he couldn't control, making the thinking choices of a victim and his performance reflected that attitude. He changed his thinking, focused on what he could control, made more positive choices and worked his way back into the first team, all through a shift in attitude. Performance follows attitude.

PUT IT INTO ACTION

- Check your attitude every day – remember that you chose it.
- If you don't like the way you're feeling, change your thinking.
- Find a 'truth-teller' in your life to help you confront reality.
- Use positive self-talk to reinforce the right attitude.

LESSON 6:

THE COMPETITION IS YOU – GET OUT OF YOUR OWN WAY

While I was on a study trip to a performance psychology conference in the USA, an American professor I was sat with told me he could teach the essence of sport psychology in one hour. He described how he introduced new students to the importance of the mind on performance. For their first lecture the students were instructed to bring trainers and to report to the gymnastics hall. They gathered round a balance beam – a 12-foot-long, 4-inch-wide piece of wood that can be set at adjustable heights from the ground. There was considerable anxiety as this was, to say the least, unexpected, and the students were meeting each other for the first time that day.

The professor told the students he was going to challenge them to walk along the beam, which was set at 2 feet off the ground, a relatively easy task. Before they started to come up to the beam, he asked them to write down the questions going through their mind. Although some were more confident than others, everybody succeeded in crossing the beam. Without commenting, the professor then set the balance beam at 4 feet – a more difficult challenge. Again, the students had to review the questions going through their mind. At this stage, four students opted out, but the rest completed the task. Finally, the professor set the beam at 6 feet from the ground and, after reviewing their mindset, the challenge was met and completed by just six students.

Having been challenged to perform in an unusual environment, the students were then set the task of collaborating and identifying the most common questions that influenced their decisions when faced by the increasing height of the beam. They reported back that there were five key questions they had faced:

1. Do I want to do this?
2. Can I do this?
3. What do others expect of me?
4. What if I fail?
5. What if I succeed?

The professor explained that the key to performance success was whether an individual could answer those questions positively in a way that allowed them to perform. If not, the individual's mind would not commit to the challenge and they would opt out. Those students, had they attempted the higher beams, might well have succeeded, but their doubts and fears were getting in their own way and preventing commitment to the challenge. The lesson that the professor illustrated with the beam exercise was teaching the students that all performance begins in the mind.

This story came immediately to mind when young Katie and her mother came to see me. Katie, a talented netball player, was highly anxious to achieve and not enjoying the process. Her mother had become concerned with Katie's mental and emotional health as she had recently run sobbing from the court after an important league game, convinced she had let herself and her team down. Katie told her mother that she had been awful, the other girls were much better players, and she was so embarrassed she did not want to carry on. However, when her mother checked in with the coaches, the conversation was about how well Katie had played.

On meeting Katie, I was impressed: she was a bright and articulate character. However, she had a strong 'internal critic' voice that constantly questioned her performance. We began the process of changing Katie's mindset by checking her performance profile, asking her to score herself out of ten for physical, technical, tactical, mental, emotional and lifestyle strengths. A picture appeared of an able and committed young athlete who scored herself low in mental and emotional areas. I then asked her to choose six words that best described her as a person and then six words that best described her as a netball player. Again, we saw a strong and confident person who then revealed a very anxious mindset when assessing herself as a performer.

When facing a challenge, the mind goes into gear first. In Katie's mind a few mistakes in that key game had overshadowed all the good aspects of her game. She assumed that the coaches – and all the other players – would have logged the mistakes. She had let her mind dwell on the negatives and felt she had not met her own high standards. By concentrating on the negatives, she got in her own way. (I return to this theme later in Lesson 8 and share the benefits of not always aiming for perfection in performance.) Her negative mindset, magnified mistake by mistake, was compounded by thoughts of what others would think about her. Confidence was dissipated, and fear of future failure held at the forefront of her mind.

Katie and I talked through the kind of questions the students had faced in the professor's lecture and over time we slowly desensitized her fear of failure. When we checked her perception of her performance against her actual play and the assessment of respected coaches, she began to understand that fear can be False Evidence Appearing Real! We worked on techniques to raise her confidence and self-esteem levels. The exercise she liked best was the 'trigger' card, where she listed the words and phrases that described her performance at its best. I call this a 'trigger' card to emphasize that you can use it as the switch to flip from negative thoughts to positive. Katie's personal trigger card read:

> I deserve to be on the court.
> This is my day.
> I am relaxed yet ready.
> My first catch and pass will be good.
> Mistakes will not deter me.
> There is nowhere else I would rather be.
> I will make this my day.

Katie read this card before every practice and game (putting it on the bathroom mirror is a good idea) and slowly changed her performer mindset from anxious to positive. Having stopped getting in her own way, she began to relax, enjoy her netball and relish her place in the team. Her maturing mental strength allowed her talent to flourish.

It is easy in sport and life to believe that dealing with the challenges we face is completely beyond our control, but there is often a you versus you element – the weak you versus the strong you, a negative mindset dominating a positive attitude. A significant proportion of my clients are, in some way or other, getting in their own way. The solution is to find and assert a positive attitude rather than dwell on the negatives. This leads us neatly on to Lesson 7.

'FIND AND ASSERT A POSITIVE ATTITUDE RATHER THAN DWELL ON THE NEGATIVES'

HOW TO GET OUT OF YOUR OWN WAY

When facing a new challenge that seems too difficult start by asking, 'Am I the problem?' Check yourself by answering these questions:

1. Do I want to do this?
2. Can I do this?
3. What do others expect of me?
4. What if I fail?
5. What if I succeed?

Compose a trigger card of phrases that describe you at your best.

Keep your trigger card handy so you can use it regularly to switch your mindset from negative to positive.

LESSON 7:

STAY POSITIVE - BE YOUR OWN CHEERLEADER

We often regard top athletes with awe, but images can often deceive. They are ordinary people doing extraordinary things, and most suffer the same doubts and fears as the rest of us.

The rugby player sat in front of me was enormous but clearly at the mercy of his anxiety. At the start of the week, he had learned that he was to play his first game for the England rugby team at Twickenham in front of 80,000 spectators and national television. This young man had been to see me that week to share his anxiety, and I knew that my work was to prevent him becoming a victim to his anxiety and to send him onto that field with a fighter mentality.

I realized that, although undoubtedly a very intelligent young man, Jeff had difficulty expressing his fears verbally. Words have enormous power, and his inability to express his feelings made it difficult for him to communicate well enough to allow me to give him the right support. I asked him to put his feelings down on paper. The evening before the game, he brought me his written efforts. As he read them, one thing immediately stood out – the repeated use of the very powerful negative word 'stressed'. At several points in his reading the player had emphasized how stressful he found the thought of playing and failing to live up to the expectations others had of him.

Confidence has been described as what we say to ourselves about what we think about ourselves. Jeff's self-talk, the conversation he was having with himself in his head, was highly negative and was therefore destroying his confidence. During the week, I had reminded him continually of his record on the rugby field and how he deserved this opportunity to shine at a national level. However, his critical inner voice was still undermining him. Unless this changed, he could not achieve release from his fears. He had to realize that stress could be converted into a positive force, challenging us to do our best work.

Negative self-talk is a difficult problem in sport, where athletes often seek an impossible level of perfection and constantly feel the fear of failure. Words determine how we feel, and the critical voice in our head can burden us with disempowering emotions: self-doubt, helplessness, confusion, fear, and so on. Positive self-talk, however, can create empowering emotions such as excitement, confidence, drive and persistence. Some believe that Barack Obama won the US presidency on the power of the words 'I can' and 'we will'.

Taking the piece of paper from Jeff, I went through it changing the word 'stressed' to 'blessed', then asked him to read the account of his anxiety again. What a difference this adjustment made, both in the way he read the piece and in the resulting shift of mindset. Negative self-talk was replaced by positive self-talk, and, since what we think determines how we feel, he became empowered to be his own cheerleader. I could see the change in him, both in the way he smiled and the way his body language changed. The word 'blessed' became his signal to change his confidence levels whenever they dipped. He left me with a smile and the words 'I can do this'. With a growing confidence in place, Jeff seized the opportunity to shine. He had an outstanding game, going on to build a successful professional career in rugby and play for England many times.

We all beat ourselves up at times and can have key negatives that we use (mine is 'useless'), but this is always a waste of time and energy. It doesn't help solve the problem. How much better and more efficient would we be if we learned to change our negative words into positive words and focused on our strengths instead of our weaknesses. A clever TV advertising campaign once showed women using a particular brand of hair colouring and declaring, 'Because I'm worth it!'

The response of the England women's football team in an exercise to boost self-confidence by reframing negative thoughts as positive is another great example. The

'BECOME YOUR OWN CHEERLEADER'

team had high anxiety and few cheerleaders and when asked to convert a selection of negative thoughts into strong, positive ones, they took some time when faced with the last question, 'Why should you not be scared on the football field?' Eventually a great answer: 'Because we'll be the toughest, meanest bitches out there!'

You can begin to retrain your mind by becoming aware and sensitive to those situations in life where you tend to become negative. Then ask yourself: why? Common reasons include anger, fatigue, boredom, frustration and despair. By appraising the situation and controlling your response you can learn to move on from such negative emotions. The key is to choose realistic and positive self-talk with words that empower and generate energy. You become your own cheerleader.

PUT IT INTO ACTION

- Become more assertive about using strong positive words like 'can' and 'will'.
- Be a cheerleader for others – it will lift your spirits.
- Seek the company of those who make you feel more positive about yourself.

LESSON 8:

RAISE YOUR BOTTOM LINE – AIM FOR MASTERY, NOT PERFECTION

One of the saddest sights I have seen is that of a young football player I worked with, Emma, sitting alone in the dressing room while her teammates celebrated an excellent win upstairs in the bar. I had become worried about Emma, a young, talented but very anxious football player, fearing the onset of depression, and I noticed her absence from the celebration. She was watching the game back on her laptop and cursing herself whenever she made an error. Her every tiny mistake became a catastrophe.

I gently suggested that every player on the field had made mistakes, and that being part of the team means being part of the celebration. In the quiet of the deserted dressing room, Emma, for the first time, shared her vulnerability. She had grown up being expected to be a top football player and to follow in the traditions of her family. Although she knew it was not really true, she felt that if she performed well, she would be loved, and if she didn't, she might not. This led to her setting very high personal goals (partly to please others) in a search for perfection. Emma confessed that when she fell short of her goals she felt guilt and shame and became very angry with herself. I persuaded Emma to rejoin the team and arranged to meet her the next day.

Perfectionism is not a behaviour but a way of thinking about yourself, where the negatives can easily drown out the positives. I had to help Emma replace her critical inner voice with a kinder and more realistic voice, such as 'All I can do is my best.' She needed to stop distorting her own story, see perfectionism as a problem, learn to lose her fear of failure, forgive her mistakes and stop overreacting to the opinions of others.

We began by discussing the impact of failure and whether she could deal with it. Emma's fear was not of losing the game, as might be first thought, but centred on matters that were rather more personal. She was very concerned about making a key mistake and being embarrassed, being criticized and letting others down. She needed to accept that the people who loved her would be there for her regardless of the outcome of her performance. The process of laying her fears on the table was the first step in helping Emma desensitize from a feeling of catastrophe and to find a confidence that, even when feeling bad, she would cope.

I then got Emma to see the big picture of her performance by watching a film clip of her direct involvement in the game, this time focusing on her positive contributions to the team performance. Slowly, we removed the knee-jerk emotional reaction to mistakes and replaced it with a different definition of success, where Emma allowed herself to feel proud of her positive contribution to the team, forgave herself the odd mistake and developed a more reasonable perception of success. To support this, I drew three lines on a flip chart. The top line represented perfection, scored at 100 per cent. I asked Emma to score her best performance and she replied '90 per cent', so the middle line was scored at 90 per cent. The next question to Emma was to assess the score for her worst performance. With a shake of her head, she replied '60 per cent.' The board looked like this.

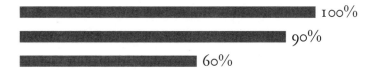

The 60 per cent performances had usually occurred when Emma made mistakes early in the game, realized she was not going to have a perfect game and compounded the first error with more mistakes. The variation from 90 per cent down to 60 per cent could really hurt the team. Emma understood and agreed to change her focus away from closing the gap from 90 per cent to 100 per cent (a worthwhile goal but a difficult and frustrating challenge) to closing the gap from 60 per cent to 90 per cent. This was a much more attainable goal that would benefit both her and the team. I stressed that changing her standards did not mean having no standards but rather having more realistic standards. Mistakes were to be seen as valuable learning opportunities and not excuses to beat herself up. This focus on 'raising the bottom line' led swiftly to a reduction in stress and anxiety and to a much-improved consistency of performance.

Alongside this process, we also had to reduce Emma's dependence on the external validation of her worthiness. She often relied on the reactions of the people in the stands and the broadcast and social media to feel good about her performance. Successful athletes performing in the public arena will be aware of the opinions of others, but their own view of themselves is what really counts – they play to their own standards.

One of the stories I told Emma was that of Jim Guymon, one of the best American basketball players to play in the UK. Jim's performances regularly reached near perfection. However, in the cup final at the end of his first season, Jim had an opportunity in the final seconds to win the game for his team. Having been fouled, Jim was awarded two foul shots, worth one point each, with one point taking the game into extra time and both points securing the win. To the amazement of all, Jim missed both shots. Interviewed on television immediately after the game, Jim said, 'In sport, as in life, sometimes you are a hero and sometimes you're a bum. Today I was a bum, tomorrow I will be a hero.'

It was no surprise that, when Jim's team won the cup the following year, he was man of the match.

Once Emma had learned to quieten her critical inner voice, to be kinder to herself and trust in her own

'RAISE YOUR BOTTOM LINE RATHER THAN SEEKING PERFECTION'

self-evaluation, she really began to enjoy and not endure her football and went from strength to strength.

In high-performance activities the drive for perfection is the ultimate intrinsic motivation. Where perfection, though desirable, is mostly unattainable there will be a constant struggle with the frustration of imperfection – no matter how good the performance is. I introduced Emma to the concept of mastery, where there is intense desire to achieve while avoiding the frustration of non-perfection. Mastery accepts that the performance might well include mistakes and setbacks but prides itself on continually striving to achieve your very best despite these. Simply put, the hard work of striving to be the best you can be (whether as an employee, a partner, a friend or a teammate) ensures that you will consistently operate on or near your 'top line' and wins you the trust of others. Could you, like Emma, embrace this and aim to raise your bottom line rather than seeking perfection?

PUT IT INTO ACTION

- Don't chase perfection – make a list of more realistic goals.
- Deal with a mistake, learn and move on.
- Set your own bar and aim for continual improvement – raise your own bar day by day.

LESSON 9:

SUCCESS IS A SERIES OF SMALL STEPS - BUILD A TICK STEPLADDER

I had heard of a young player called Evan before the manager of the football club brought him to see me. Physically, technically and tactically, he was an above-average player, but he was decidedly below average in attitude and behaviour. Evan was generally regarded as a decent young man, though one who was struggling to escape the bad habits ingrained by his background. He was not being difficult deliberately, it was simply that his life so far had not prepared him. It was a case 'that he did not know what he did not know'. As an act of desperation before releasing him, the manager handed Evan over to me with a three-week ultimatum. If Evan did not change, then he would be gone. The task was threefold – change Evan's mindset and thus his motivation so he could create new and more acceptable behavioural habits.

The first thing I established with Evan was what he wanted – his reason why. Why he wanted to win, why he wanted to play football and simply why he got up every morning. He was very passionate about being a professional player. He realized he was in the 'last chance saloon' and agreed that he must change. The problem was that such a change would have to be very significant and might be too much for Evan to conceive and implement. It's tempting to try to overhaul everything at once, but patience is the key. Taking more time to gradually implement small changes that can be applied consistently over the long term will always be more sustainable than a big change that can only be adhered to for a short period.

So, each day over the twenty-one days that the manager had allowed us, Evan and I worked on a single small and doable action. Players had to be on the field ready to train by 10:30 a.m., but for Evan, the original 'lastminute.com' person, this was usually a struggle, and he was often the last player to make it. On day one, Evan's behaviour change was to be on time, with a simple instruction to arrive no later than 9:30 a.m. I made it clear that if he failed he would be handed back to the manager. The next day, Evan arrived at the club at 9:30 a.m. and was fully prepared for the training session, where he performed well. That afternoon, I gave Evan his next doable action – get a haircut! I explained to him that if you look good you feel good and you play good. The next day, Evan arrived even earlier with a smart haircut. The third morning, he arrived early, looked smart and proceeded to shake hands and wish good morning to all the people he met. By now Evan's changed behaviour was producing a positive reaction from the people around him. Day by day he was building a personal lifestyle and professional discipline with habits that allowed him to feel more confident about his role in the club. He was building up a 'tick stepladder' and discovering that small successes are fun, that people around him responded more positively, and these reactions were motivating him to stay with the process.

For three weeks we increased Evan's awareness of who he could be and what he could achieve, each day introducing a behavioural change that improved him personally and professionally. From timekeeping – be first out to practice – to appearance – dress like a professional and role model – to communication – listening attentively when others are speaking – to relationships – becoming a valuable team member – and finally to leadership – showing initiative and taking responsibility. Evan was learning that true strength of character is the ability to do the next right thing over and over again.

Admiral William H. McRaven also writes in his book *Make Your Bed* about little things that can change your world:

> If you make your bed every morning, you will have accomplished your first task of the day. It will give you a small sense of pride and it will encourage you to do another task and another and another. By the end of the day that one task completed will have turned into many tasks completed. Making your bed will also reinforce the fact that little things in life matter. If you can't do little things right, you will never do the big things right.

At the end of that three-week development pro-gramme, the manager was quite happy for Evan to remain in the senior squad. Two years later, he became the cap-tain and built a very successful career as a professional player. We understand that good character brings effective action, but in Evan's case effective action brought good character.

Jenny was a young under-16 basketball player whose problem was not that she was getting in her own way, but rather that her mother was. Jenny was not achieving the success that her talent indicated. After ten minutes of meeting Jenny and her mother, I understood why. Every time I asked Jenny a question she would look over to her mother, who would take over the response. Her mother was persuaded that her daughter could only grow into her talent if she showed more responsibility and self-discipline. We planned a series of small steps that Jenny's mother would let Jenny complete alone. Each one – making her bed, packing her own kit bag, managing her timekeeping, controlling her relationship with her coach, and so on, was easily doable. However, taken together, this stepladder of good habits gave Jenny significant momentum towards becoming a self-managing athlete. Her confidence and assertiveness soared, and she began to show her undoubted talent on the basketball court.

There are times in life when change is necessary, though we all appreciate change can be very difficult, especially changing our own behaviour. It can be made

'PLAN A SERIES OF SMALL STEPS LEADING TOWARDS THE EVENTUAL GOAL'

more achievable if you plan a series of small steps leading towards the eventual goal. Envisage this as a 'tick stepladder' that allows the build-up of relatively easy successes, thus building confidence to see the change through. Start this process by working from the end backwards, asking yourself what would represent success, then breaking this down into the steps necessary to achieve it, creating small doable actions. Each step forward rewards you with a 'tick' towards your end goal. If you have the discipline to follow your programme, then, like Evan and Jenny, you will have given yourself the best chance of success.

PUT IT INTO ACTION

- Determine what success would look like for you.
- Plan a series of small steps to get there.
- Focus on achieving each step, one by one.
- Give yourself a pat on the back when you tick one off.

LESSON 10:

DEFINE THE MOMENT - OR THE MOMENT WILL DEFINE YOU

A couple of years ago, my son asked me to write the story of my life. As I began tracing back through the years, most of it represented steady progress: education, building a career, enjoying sport, creating a family, and so on. However, I realized there were maybe a dozen critical moments that had greatly influenced my life. Although I deeply regretted the moments where I was found wanting, there were enough moments when I seized the opportunity and shaped my future successfully.

Becoming a performance psychologist in sport was not a first intention. I was very happy as a basketball player and then coaching a National League team alongside my teaching career. I became increasingly aware of the power of psychology while coaching the England men's team. The moment that changed everything for me came one evening in Christchurch, New Zealand, when our England team was playing the host team in the semi-final of the Commonwealth Championships. England had never won a medal in basketball, and victory that night would guarantee silver or gold (no bronze medals would be awarded), so this was a very big moment for us.

With twenty seconds left on the clock, we trailed New Zealand by one point and had possession of the ball for the final shot to win the game. The team on court went into a well-rehearsed play that would guarantee our best shooter, Brian, would take the final shot – the 'money' shot. Everything worked beautifully, and with the seconds ticking away Brian had the ball in a position well within his range. With the passionate New Zealand home crowd on their feet, he shocked us all. He didn't shoot – instead passing the ball to a teammate. Like the rest of our staff and players I was stunned and watched as a surprised player took a difficult shot. He missed, and the ball was rebounded by a New Zealand player. Then, in an amazing act of resilience, our captain forced the rebounder to step over the line. We were awarded the ball back with five seconds left in the game.

I immediately called a time-out – saved for such a situation. Three of the players facing me would not make eye contact. The decision on who should take the final shot was made for me when Tony, a tall, long-haired, relaxed individual who had only scored two from eleven shots in the game, put his arm around me and told me he had dreamed of this moment and I could trust him. I organized a simple move to get the ball to Tony. With two seconds left on the clock he scored a magnificent long-range shot. We were through to the final and went on to win the gold medal!

That twenty seconds in the semi-final taught me the importance of mental strength on performance under pressure: Brian choking on the shot, our captain never giving up and winning the ball back, and Tony taking responsibility and delivering the win. Like many coaches, I had been fascinated by talent and had not fully realized that, whilst a level of talent is essential, so is the power of the mind to shape that talent successfully. The captain and Tony defined their key moments in the game, and Brian was defined by his.

Brian and I met the next day. What followed was a fascinating conversation with a pleasant young man, a very talented athlete who suffered from one flaw in his mental strength. We discussed the fear that lay behind his decision not to take the final shot of the game. His explanation was that the combined pressure of expectations, consequences, the New Zealand home crowd and the media sideshow proved too much for him. His mental strength did not match the moment. The real bravery in sport lies in wanting the ball when the game is on the line.

Brian was, of course, focusing on things that cannot be controlled and needed help to concentrate instead on those things he had control over. We discussed his experience of similar situations, his specific preparation, his excellent shooting record and the confidence his teammates and the coaches had in him. The real key, however, was in Brian understanding that occasional failure is the price of accepting the challenge, and that for an elite athlete the ability to define the moment will always outweigh the cost of passively letting the moment define you. We discussed recovery strategies from such a miss, and then I ended the session by reminding Brian that the next evening we were playing for a gold medal, and, if it came down to the final shot, I would expect him to be willing to take it. In the event England won by a decent margin, and the situation did not materialize.

The final shot situation is an ever-present challenge to high-performers in many sports. There is perhaps no more mentally and emotionally demanding moment in sport than taking part in a penalty shootout at the end of the game. An example I use with athletes today is the women's field hockey final at the 2016 Rio Olympic Games, where Great Britain beat the reigning champions the Netherlands 2–0 in a thrilling penalty shootout after drawing 3–3 in normal time. Hollie Pearne-Webb defined the moment of the vital final penalty goal for GB and later reflected in the media on her mental state: 'I reminded myself I could do this. I kept recalling that I had done this many times before. I walked slowly up, showing I was in control. I looked as confident as I could and stood really tall. Finally, I looked the goalkeeper in the eye.'

Simple thoughts and actions but very powerful in sending a message both to herself and to the goalkeeper: 'I am going to do this!'

'OCCASIONAL FAILURE IS THE PRICE OF ACCEPTING THE CHALLENGE'

PUT IT INTO ACTION

In designing and writing your own life story of who you want to be and how you want to live, there will be moments when you will be challenged. Don't let them become 'should'a, could'a, would'a' memories, leaving you reflecting on what might have been.

- Recognize such moments.
- Take responsibility.
- Define the situation rather than being defined by it.
- Accept the price of growth may sometimes be failure.

LESSON 11:

FOCUS ON THE PROCESS – LET THE WINS COME TO YOU

I was at home watching the news, when an interview with a young woman who had just won two Olympic gold medals came on. The interviewer pointed to the two gold medals around the athlete's neck and commented that she had been rewarded for chasing them. Instantly, she replied that she had not chased any medals, she had trained six hours a day every day for years and those medals came to her. The interviewer went on to praise her sacrifice. She was insistent that there was no sacrifice, she had chosen to train six hours a day. Her responses stand as the very model of a champion's mindset.

At the time, I was helping Steve, a young swimmer who was desperate to become a champion. He had enjoyed some early success in his career, tasted and relished the celebrity that goes with it. He definitely had the talent and the ability to work hard to become a champion, but the closer he got to any competitive event, the more he lost emotional control and discipline. Unlike the athlete described above, he began to chase the wins and lost attention and control of the essential process, the day-to-day preparation, that would give him success.

Steve's mindset was dominated by the desire to win and gain recognition. So much so that his focus, the ability to be in the present and stay in the now, disappeared and he lost the concentration to train effectively. He was locked into outcomes that he could not control and thus wasted time and energy, sabotaging himself from becoming the champion he desired to be. Steve's goal was to win, but he needed to learn to 'park' this ambition once set, then turn his attention to focusing on the aspects of his preparation that he could control. I needed Steve to understand that true recognition for an athlete comes after a long period of hard work.

I shared with him my first week working at Manchester United. Watching the team training on my first day, I realized immediately that the commitment, focus and intensity was higher than anything I had come across before. The second day provided another lesson. The weather was absolutely foul, but in the dressing room before practice a shout was heard: 'Rainy Tuesday morning, boys – step up.' Despite the weather the practice was excellent, and later the captain explained that champions train every day like champions whatever the weather – no excuses! When game time came around on the Saturday, the players were completely relaxed, and the captain confirmed, 'We work hard Monday to Friday to give us the best chance of enjoying Saturday.'

Steve began to understand that dreaming of victory

was not going to help him unless it translated into daily positive actions. To help him achieve and maintain daily momentum, we decided each evening he would write down six actions that he would commit to achieve the following day. This habitual discipline worked well, and gradually he began to make more of the daily opportunities that build the mindset of potential champions. Mentally, he was transforming from a focus on emotion-laden outcome to concentration on the everyday process of becoming excellent. Finally, Steve was able to deal with the pressures of elite competition by remaining in the present instead of his mind racing ahead to victory. Happily, Steve finally achieved the success he sought.

As we near the climax of every football and rugby season, sport psychologists await the phone calls from coaches of teams closing in on success or failure. It's a decisive moment when a coach wrestles for control of their team's mindset. The conversations in and around the team will be about likely outcomes. If this is allowed to take over, focus on the process of preparation can diminish. As Dawn Peart, the hugely experienced and long-serving British swimming team manager, once told me, 'Most people want to be in the result and not the process. However, it's in the process when you realize who deserves to be in the result.'

One such phone call came from the manager of a Football League team that for two seasons had led the league table up to the closing stages, only to fade away and miss promotion. For a third season the team found

'CONCENTRATE ON THE EVERYDAY PROCESS OF BECOMING EXCELLENT'

itself in a similar position. Again, the possibility of great success began influencing their mindset. My task was to help change the conversation and ensure focus on their daily agenda. I asked the team in which sport did the participants never see the finishing line. We agreed it was rowing and discussed what impact that would have. Obviously, rowers can only focus on the quality of each stroke, maintaining the quality of the process and as a result aim to finish strongly. The team understood the message, focused on the quality of their daily practice, ignored promotion 'hype' and achieved their ambition.

PUT IT INTO ACTION

It's good to set outcome goals that stretch and inspire you, but you cannot let them distract you from the process of building the skills that allow you to achieve them. Wanting to achieve is good but remains simply a desire. You have to turn intention into action by working hard on becoming better every single day.

- 'Park' your goal and focus on the now.
- List several actions to be achieved each day.
- Perform these tasks as well as you can.

If you have sufficient application, you will be surprised how often the wins will come to you.

LESSON 12:

SELF-CONTROL IS THE KEY – DON'T BE CAPTIVE TO YOUR EMOTIONS

For the elite performer competing in the arena, some stress is inevitable, and emotional control can become a winning characteristic. Novak Djokovic demonstrated this at the Wimbledon tennis championships, when at the last moment he was forced to play a match without his cap, having been told it did not meet the dress code. This was despite the world number one having worn the same cap the match before. In this situation Novak could have lost control. However, his response was, 'I just accepted it and dealt with it.' He stayed in control and that year went on to become the singles champion.

A common issue that I've seen in young athletes is when they let their emotions control their behaviour rather than being in control of their emotions. Ben was a very promising young golfer though he had a tendency to collapse in the second half of a round. Walking the course and observing his performance, I noticed that his attitude dipped around the ninth hole. When we discussed what he was thinking and how he was feeling, this downward negative spiral became obvious. At about the ninth hole Ben made his first estimate of what his final score might be based on his current score, and if it wasn't what he'd planned for, negative emotions kicked in and disempowered him for the rest of the round. Once we had identified the problem, we were able to work together to find a solution. Ben would take a break at the end of the ninth hole, have a snack to boost his energy, some water to rehydrate and reset his mindset with the challenge that the second half of the round would be better than the first. This proved very effective in helping him 'park' his score after nine holes and start the last nine holes with fresh hope and energy, leading to better and more consistent performances.

A first step in building emotional control is to check for any underlying conditions that might be stressing you. I teach athletes to check themselves against the acronym HATED:

H – Hungry
A – Angry (or Alcohol)
T – Tired
E – Emotional
D – Dehydrated

Any of these can be a condition that makes for a greater susceptibility to loss of control and subsequently bring regret for the ensuing behaviour. If these basic factors are taken care of, then there is a better chance of controlling your mind and your emotions when faced by difficult circumstances. The next step is to develop a coping strategy, using tactics that work in your particular context.

This was illustrated some years ago when the manager of a national youth football team came to me for help to minimize the risks of the following potential situation. The team had been drawn away from home in the European Championships to play a country whose football supporters at the time were notoriously and vocally racist. Our likely starting team featured three black players. In theoretical football terms we should have had no problem in winning the game, but if we couldn't handle the emotional pressure built up by noisy and abusive spectators, we might very well lose. We formulated a strategy to reduce the risk of losing our cool and giving the opposition an advantage, help to empower our players and ensure best possible emotional control throughout the team.

At a meeting with the players and the staff prior to travelling, we talked through our perceptions of what might happen and the different ways the players could interpret such situations. For example, we agreed that probably only a small percentage of the crowd would actually shout racist comments. (Thankfully, such racist abuse is now universally condemned and much, much less common in today's game.) Then we discussed how our team could talk themselves and each other into an emotionally controlled and positive response while out on the field. Finally, we agreed that this was all very well in a classroom but the winning behaviour we wanted had to take place in the heat of battle, so I gave our players a 'trigger phrase' on which they could anchor their response. I asked them what the different colours mean at traffic lights. Everybody knows that green means go, red means stop and amber means get ready for a change. We decided the winning colour for us would be the steady flow of green and 'seeing red' was to be avoided at all costs. Amber was very important as a warning sign to a possible change of state. The players left the room with a clear message: 'Stay in the green.'

On match night, whenever one or more of the team felt the onset of 'amber', our trigger phrase was to be heard loud and clear from the players (and staff), and self-control was able to be re-established. In the dressing room, the tunnel before the game and throughout the game 'Stay in the green' was communicated individually and collectively. Despite severe provocation, emotions were controlled, and behaviour remained focused and disciplined. We played disciplined football, dealt with the intimidation, and the result was a 3–0 victory.

For much of my life I have been captive to my emotions. When challenged, whether in sport or in life, my emotions would kick in, often overwhelming me and ruling out the possibility of a rational response. These emotional surges would disempower me, bringing self-doubt, fear, insecurity and helplessness. I wasted a lot of

'TAKE CARE
OF YOUR OWN
PHYSICAL AND
EMOTIONAL
STATE'

time and effort to no effect. Life can prove very difficult at times and we all say and do things that we regret later. Staying in control and refusing to be captive to our emotions is an important habit in building a mature and winning mindset.

If you take care of your own physical and emotional state and interpret any situation before you, checking the evidence in a more careful, controlled manner, you can deal with things rather than react, and your emotions will become empowering rather than disempowering. When successful give yourself a pat on the back for your emotional resilience in dealing and not reacting to difficult situations.

PUT IT INTO ACTION

The 'traffic lights' strategy can help most people in many situations when emotions are challenging rational thought. The important things to remember are:

- Accept the challenge – see challenge and not threat.
- Prepare – anticipate those situations that cause you to lose control.
- Focus on the outcome – decide what you want to happen.

- Enjoy being in the 'green' – in control and making progress.
- Recognize 'amber' – feel the loss of control and snap back to 'green'.
- Avoid 'red' – a non-productive state that will harm progress and relationships.

LESSON 13:

DEFEAT YOUR ANXIETY –
EMBRACE THE CHALLENGE

A simple choice determines whether athletes perform at their best when it really counts or fall apart under the expectations of others and fear of failure. Do they see the competition as a threat or a challenge?

When Paul, a seventeen-year-old football player of great promise at a small lower league club, was asked by the manager if he was ready for the first team he replied, 'Boss, I was born ready.' However, as match day got closer, Paul's anxiety grew and I knew he wasn't ready. On the day before the game, Paul confessed to me he was worried about playing in front of a large crowd. Even though we were playing at home, Paul saw the crowd as a threat. The manager and I realized that this state of anxiety could undermine Paul's confidence and destroy his performance. The manager bravely allowed me to try an idea.

When Paul reported for the match, I told him to put a tracksuit on and follow me. We walked to the side of the pitch and, despite his visible discomfort, we started to walk around in front of the spectators. The crowd was mostly made up of families who had arrived early for the game. Every so often I would stop and talk to a group of fans and Paul began to realize that they were not a threat but a support group wanting the team – and him – to do well. His anxiety lessened, Paul had a very good game and went on to become a first-team regular.

When being challenged to perform to a high standard there will always be those situations that create some anxiety. The situations themselves are not necessarily the problem, it's how we interpret them and add our own negative meaning that leads to an anxious response. Paul initially saw the crowd as a threat that could lead to his embarrassment, humiliation, shame and being viewed as worthless. Once he had met some of the spectators and changed his interpretation of the situation from negative to positive, he became challenged to do well for them and his energy, confidence and focus were all raised.

The key to managing anxiety is to get beyond the initial emotional reaction and check the evidence. My advice is to remember that feelings, however strong they are, are not facts. Asking questions of yourself, such as: Is this really a threat? What's the worst that could happen? means we assemble facts. Marshalling such evidence means that you can reinterpret what appeared to be a stressful situation as a challenge and not a threat.

During the week that followed that game Paul and I met to reinforce this new mental strength. Like all athletes, he loved stories, whether from real life or drawn from books and films, about how other high performers cope with their challenges. One film we discussed was *A League of Their Own*, a fictionalized account based on an actual situation in the USA when women baseball teams replaced the regular men's teams during the Second World War. At first the move was met with scepticism and the women played to small crowds. However, they began to improve and, along with the shortage of sporting entertainment, began to attract larger crowds. One of the players, Dottie, emerged as a 'star' and she in particular felt the pressure of the increase in expectations. For the first time she felt that what began as a challenge had suddenly become a threat and she worried about the consequences and embarrassment of failure. In a key scene in the film, Dottie, played by Geena Davis, goes to see the manager, played by Tom Hanks, and tells him she is quitting. When he asks her why she tells him that it has become 'too tough'. His response is a coaching classic: 'It's supposed to be hard. If it wasn't hard, everyone would do it. The hard is what makes it great.' This influences Dottie's mindset and she moves from seeing only threat to accepting the challenge.

Players and teams can find anxiety in failure and success as both can be difficult to deal with. I have used this story many times with teams because it paints a recognizable picture of the threat of external pressures that athletes can face. The message of the story, that facing challenge is tough but you can deal with it, translated perfectly in the response from a women's soccer team at a college in the USA when, following my showing them the film clips, they all turned up at practice the next week wearing T-shirts with the message 'We Do Tough'.

There are many stories about coping with fear in sport and life. They emphasize that dealing with our anxieties depends on calmly checking the evidence, assessing risk and, where acceptable, pushing forward to deal with the situation ahead. Over time, this approach builds the mental strength to interpret situations as a challenge and not as a threat. The experience accumulated gives the confidence to cope with initial fear in more new situations.

We must accept that some degree of anxiety can be useful. It is a helpful signal that can keep us safe from potentially harmful situations. Where appropriate and controlled, anxiety can drive us to higher levels of performance and greater success. The key is in changing from emotional helplessness, 'I can't deal with this', to thinking through valid options thus creating belief in yourself, 'this is tough but I can deal with it.' The more you do this the less likely you are to suffer an emotional overreaction that blocks you dealing with the issue. There will be some failure along the way, which you must learn to accept, be proud you tried, learn what to do better next time and move on. As always, the choice is yours, but just think what a difference it would make to your life if, like Paul, you decide to face the challenge head on and always choose grit not quit.

'CHOOSE GRIT NOT QUIT'

PUT IT INTO ACTION

Imagine a situation that you know will be fearful for you and play out this 'What If . . . Then . . .' process:

- Assess your options.
- Write down all the possible consequences, starting with 'What's the worst that could happen?'
- Assess the likelihood (the risk) of each consequence.
- Finally, choose the solution that works best for you.

Remember the process with the acronym SOCS:

Situation
Options
Consequences
Solution

LESSON 14:

REFUSE TO BE A VICTIM – DEVELOP RESILIENCE FROM SETBACKS

It's more than thirty years since I coached the England basketball team, and over the years the captain Paul Stimpson has stayed in contact with me. During one of our conversations Paul reminded me that when we were defeated in our first game, walking together from the arena, I'd suggested that the captain ought to be first to our practice session the next day. If the captain refused to be a victim and fought back, then the team would be more likely to follow. High performance brings a constant challenge and the associated threat that sometimes we will fail to meet our own expectations and those of others. This is a crucial moment that defines the journey to success for many people. The key is refusing to be a victim and staying in the game.

When suffering mentally and emotionally from a setback, very often the biggest asset a player has is their partner at home. When Chris, a highly talented rugby player, broke his leg, it was his wife, Lynn, who was key to his recovery. Everybody at the club knew what a setback this was for Chris after he'd fought so hard to make the first team. It was Lynn who, in a phone call, alerted us to the extent of Chris's shock, anger and lack of desire to begin the process of recovery. She described his inability to move on as a state of mental paralysis. On visiting Chris at home, I listened carefully without judgement as Chris expressed the anger and hurt he felt. This was key to the start of his healing process. Without this release Chris could not progress to coping with his emotions and onwards to problem solving.

Our next step was to move Chris from avoidance to acceptance, eliminating blame and changing his mental state from being locked into the past to focusing on now and the future. This involved helping Chris understand that setbacks are part of the challenge when aiming for high performance, then reframing the situation as a possible opportunity to come back stronger and not a threat to his playing future. Again, Lynn intervened very helpfully. She produced a wall calendar she had designed for the kitchen that showed the timeline of Chris's recovery with every potential date marked up with the stages of recovery given them by the club doctor and physiotherapists. Chris could clearly see how many days it would be until he could begin walking, swimming, riding a bicycle, light training and then rejoining the team. They would mark off every day before dinner and decided together that their aim was to shorten the process by one week by working hard on rehabilitation.

Gradually we were dealing with less emotion, more

information, and Chris was redirecting his emotional energy to positive purposes. Another significant moment was when Chris asked, 'How can I come back better?' Many people are able to heal, though fail to see the situation as a significant learning moment when they can reset their skills and behavioural patterns. Chris began to see a series of small successes, his confidence grew, and as Lynn predicted he returned to the team one week earlier than the experts had predicted. Shortly after, he was back in the first team and has gone on to have a long and successful career.

Tom was a regular starter for his football league team and, like Chris, suffered a setback. He was suddenly dropped from the team to the bench as a substitute and reacted badly. I could see from his body language and behaviour at practice that he was becoming a classic victim. Our first conversation allowed him to release his emotions, our second dealt with the excuses and blaming. Tom, a sincere and thoughtful young man, began to accept responsibility. Slowly we moved Tom's mindset from victim to fighter mentality. He realigned what he'd felt as criticism into a challenge to perform better when any opportunity arose. We began to discuss how he would behave as a substitute in the coming game, illustrated with the example of Ole Gunnar Solskjaer.

A supremely talented player, Ole Gunnar spent much of his career at Manchester United as a substitute and became famous as a player who could come onto the field late in the game and make a positive, often winning, impact. (The most well-remembered illustration of this is the 1999 European Champions Cup final when Ole Gunnar scored United's winning goal in extra time.) Being a substitute is not easy for a player, but Ole Gunnar created a mindset of complete positivity, stayed totally focused and engaged in the game as it played out on the pitch, and so was fully prepared mentally and physically when the manager put him into the game.

Once Tom had absorbed this model of an 'impact' substitute, his attitude and behaviour changed. In the next game, when he came onto the field for the last twenty minutes, he had a clear picture of his role, brought energy and determination and changed the game in his team's favour (though not the final result)! His performance put him right back into contention for the starting line-up in the next game.

Chris and Tom each became more aware of how they had initially allowed their emotions to take over after a setback, clouding their ability to capture any learning and make progress. Their experiences led to new understanding, that setbacks are temporary, to be regretted. However, if they are followed up by learning ('What should I have done differently?', 'How would I deal with a similar situation next time?'), then bouncing back positively creates resilience and mental toughness to face future situations. Their choice was between getting frustrated or getting fascinated with the process of improving. Both players

'WE ALL SUFFER SETBACKS AND FAILURES IN OUR LIVES BUT WE MUST NOT ACCEPT THEM AS PERSONAL OR PERMANENT' learned to 'park' their frustration on an imaginary shelf, work hard and focus on what's next.

A significant element of my work has been helping teams and individuals who are going through difficult setbacks. The process is invariably the same, beginning with checking for victim signs – finding excuses or blaming, not accepting feedback or criticism, resisting learning and change, hiding under pressure and accepting average performance. The mind is the key battlefield, and my job in such situations is to assist in changing minds from the paralysis of denial to the positive possibilities of recovery.

We all suffer setbacks and failures in our lives but we must not accept them as personal or permanent. Far better to see them as a challenge to be overcome and look for the learning so that we can emerge from that process stronger and more resilient with the experience to deal with future setbacks.

PUT IT INTO ACTION

When next faced with an unfortunate situation try to follow the guidelines that helped Chris, Tom and many others:

- Accept that some failure is part of the journey and do not be deterred.
- Overcome your negative emotions.

- Pride yourself on your resilience and get started on a recovery plan of action.
- Learn from every setback and emerge a stronger person.

LESSON 15:

BUILD A SUPPORT TEAM – FEED OFF THE STRENGTH OF OTHERS

The basketball team at the University of Florida agreed on the concept of FAMILY (Forget About Me I Love You). When the team won the National Championship this was stress-tested when the star, Joakim Noah, was offered the honour of appearing on the front cover of *Sports Illustrated* (this premier US sports magazine only offers this front-cover opportunity to a very few top performers, such as Michael Jordan). His response was 'Not without my guys,' and the team was featured on the front cover. Similarly, when Joakim was invited into Basketball's Hall of Fame, his reply was 'Not without my guys,' and the team made the Hall of Fame together. It is not difficult to imagine how such a level of mutual support led to winning performances from each individual.

When Caroline, a women's football coach at a US college, met her newly assembled squad for the first time, she organized a squad photograph. After a few days getting to know each other, she invited all the players to a pizza party at her home. After food, drink and games, she asked the squad to work together to complete a jigsaw that she had made featuring the squad photo-graph. However, Caroline kept back one piece featuring a player's face. All the squad enjoyed the collective activ-ity but were frustrated by the lack of that one piece. She let them absorb the significance of this for a while and then produced the missing piece. She discussed with them how they felt when one of the team was excluded and how they felt when the squad was complete. Imagine how the player who was not in the picture felt: isolated, unloved and not needed, and how much better she felt when back in the picture as part of the team.

Caroline was creating a psychological safety zone for her young players, an individual and collective support system. She realized that they might not be able to deal with the challenge of competition alone and needed to know that support was available. The exercise with the jigsaw was a way of showing that no one should be left isolated and the team and the coaches together were a mutually supportive unit. Players could say 'I need help' without feeling weak or embarrassed. When I started pioneering applied sport psychology, I was sometimes the only psychological safety zone available to players to confess they had a problem. Expressing an issue that could be perceived as a weakness by the coach was not an option for these athletes. Having the courage to express vulnerability to another person is the start of building an effective support team.

Watching Caroline shape the collective psychology of

her team helped me when faced with a major problem affecting a women's basketball team. Although this team had been successful and qualified for a major tournament, trust and relationships had broken down. The support system for the players had been damaged as the coaches had concentrated exclusively on performance and forgotten the importance of relationships. For example, some players reported that the coaches had not had any personal conversations with them. The coaches were treating the players as 'human doings' and not as 'human beings'. The women no longer accepted a leadership that was solely task-focused and that showed no personal respect or concern for their welfare. To help salvage the situation, the administrators let the coaches go, appointed a young coach and assistant and asked me to help them turn around the situation.

I asked for a meeting with coaches and support staff the day before the team reported back, and when we got together, I set the staff an exercise. They were to work together to identify five ways in which they could make the players feel needed, then cared for, listened to and finally appreciated. We filled a flip chart with their twenty responses. If the staff could rebuild relationships using these actions as a basis, the players could rediscover their enthusiasm and commitment.

Once the team returned and we had shared time together, I asked them to divide into pairs and explained the concept of belief partners. Belief partners are committed to each other's development as athletes; they always stress the positives, constantly inject confidence and intervene when they see their partner behaving in a negative way that could undermine performance. As part of that responsibility, they were to carry out an act of kindness for their partner every day that the team was together. At the end-of-tournament debrief a number of the players commented on the morale-boosting impact of being treated to a coffee, receiving small gifts or simply having someone showing personal care and attention.

All these initiatives gave the team new spirit, and an improved performance followed. Moving from feeling unloved and uncared for, now the players were sur-rounded by a positive support group. Feeling needed, cared for, listened to, appreciated and being supported by a trusted belief partner gave the team members a strong and positive emotional basis to their perform-ance. That tournament proved the best run of results that team had ever produced.

Sport can be a very cruel business, and the dressing room after a defeat is a sad place to be. The whole squad and staff have to learn to support each other in those moments. When the England under-21 football team defeated Ireland in the European Championships in Cyprus, I was naturally delighted though also aware of how disappointed the Irish boys were. A couple of hours after the game, three of the English players came to my hotel room to take me to see how the Irish team was sharing the pain. They were sat round the small pool at the hotel, legs dangling in the water, while the team doctor played guitar and they sang traditional Irish songs together. It is easier to face the pain of life's difficulties if we can share them together.

Our journey through life can be very challenging, even more so when we try to do it alone. It is far better to build a support group with family, friends and work colleagues so that, just like the basketball team or that young Irish football team, you can draw on their strength when needed. Have the courage to reach out to the communities you belong to, share your vulnerabilities and build mutually supportive relationships.

Modern lifestyle and work patterns often determine that we live alone for some periods of our life. It is easy to get isolated, depressed, out of touch and slowly lose our support group. You must, like the teams I have described, learn that increasing communication decreases anxiety, confirming 'a problem only exists in the absence of a good conversation'. Reaching out and nurturing relationships with your family and friends can become part of your daily discipline. It can be wonderful what a supportive phone call can do to raise mood and morale.

'INCREASING COMMUNICATION DECREASES ANXIETY'

PUT IT INTO ACTION

- Identify the members of your support group.
- Don't be afraid to say 'I need help.'
- Ask yourself what you can do for each of them.
- Keep in regular contact and share meaningful conversations.

LESSON 16:

CONTROL YOUR BANDWIDTH – PRIORITIZE WHAT COUNTS

'You don't really understand, Bill,' cried Melissa as she jumped to her feet. I was working with the freshman members of the women's soccer team at an American university, exploring the challenges of dealing with their first year at college. Melissa, an eighteen-year-old medical student who was also an outstanding soccer player, came up to the front. She then described her freshman year by demonstrating the process of spinning plates on the end of a cane. As she set the first imaginary plate spinning, she said it represented how tough she was finding the academic work. The second plate reflected how challenging she was finding the soccer programme. The third plate Melissa described as the pressure of her mother calling her several times every day. She now acted out that the first plate was wobbling and about to fall so she had to go back and give that an extra spin. The fourth plate was the fact that her boyfriend from home was visiting that coming weekend, and (to great laughter) the fifth was that her boyfriend at college did not want him to. By now, Melissa was running up and down the imaginary plates spinning for her life and then she pretended that they all crashed. 'Bill,' she said, 'that's what my life feels like at the moment!'

In a creative and entertaining way, Melissa had described how her personal bandwidth was out of control. I explained to the team that their personal bandwidth was the number of situations, whether personal, social or work-related, that they could deal with before losing focus and feeling overwhelmed. Melissa was trying to deal with too many situations at once and trying to be all things to all people. Everybody differs in their physical, mental and emotional capacity to deal with situations. The discussion that followed revealed that many of the student players felt they were at times overwhelmed, ineffective, making too many mistakes and seeing problems too late. At first, they claimed lack of time, but as the discussion went on, this changed to a lack of the energy required to focus on the main areas that mattered in their lives. Issues then emerged such as unrealistic goals, poor control of schedules, not getting enough sleep and too much time on their phones and social media.

At this point, one of the team described her life as a marathon. Together, we explored the concept that for people like them who wanted to live life as student high-performers it was not a marathon but a series of sprints. To deal with the challenges of academic work, sport and relationships in an effective manner required energy – enough energy to apply the proper focus and attention to the priority task or activity in order to produce a peak performance moment that could best be described as a sprint. However, if each sprint were not followed by an appropriate recovery time, then the next sprint would have insufficient energy to operate at maximum level. Without proper recovery to replenish energy very soon, their performance could be described as 'running on empty'. The players were fascinated. Since arriving at college the whole conversation had been about work – nobody had mentioned rest and recovery, never mind actually recommending it! Similarly, no one had spoken about the value of prioritization and keeping their commitments simple.

For some high-performers success can bring problems. One of my long-standing clients, Brad, was so successful and received so many wonderful offers that his personal bandwidth expanded completely out of control. To recover the situation, Brad and I went back to basics. We agreed that he had to set boundaries around his bandwidth to ensure effectiveness, quality of life and balance. After some considerable time identifying what he wanted from life and setting realistic goals, we refocused on building his bandwidth around personal and professional success. Here it is represented as a continuum.

?	FAMILY	FITNESS AND HEALTH	CAREER AND FINANCE	?
OPTIONAL	PRIORITY	ESSENTIAL	PRIORITY	OPTIONAL

Brad prioritized being fit and healthy, maintaining solid family and personal relationships, having a stimulating career and being comfortable financially. We agreed his successful bandwidth – and happiness – would be maintaining a balance across those non-negotiable goals and having the courage to say no to unnecessary commitments. Brad has developed the discipline to make the right choices, a rationale for saying no, and life has become simpler, happier and more successful for him.

If you balance your rest and recovery with work and activity output, you will find you have the energy to attack the important things with your full focus and considerably improve your chances of success. As the late Steve Jobs said, 'That's been one of my mantras – focus and simplicity. Simple can be harder than complex – you have to work hard to get your thinking clean to make it simple. But it's worth it in the end because once you get there, you can move mountains.'

'DEVELOP THE DISCIPLINE TO MAKE THE RIGHT CHOICES'

PUT IT INTO ACTION

- Check your bandwidth whenever you feel overwhelmed, ineffective or are making too many mistakes.
- Clearly establish what you want and the priorities for action.
- Keep tight control of your schedule and say no to the things that don't really matter.

LESSON 17:

DO THE RIGHT THING – AND BE ACCOUNTABLE FOR YOUR ACTIONS

There are certain non-negotiables that have to be accepted when committing to a team. It is only right that team members are expected to be on time, be prepared, listen and learn, do a good job, be good teammates and so on. Most athletes understand this and, providing the programme of work is purposeful, inclusive and stimulating, they will accept and fall into line. However, I was working with a Premier League football manager who insisted there must be a set of published rules, accompanied by sanctions, covering all behavioural infringements. I suggested as an alternative we should have the one key guideline: that the players were expected to 'do the right thing' in all situations. This would place the ownership and responsibility for their behaviour onto the athletes themselves. Any deviations would provide good teaching and learning situations. This worked excellently, and we only had a few problems. Upbringing, education and instinct should drive us towards understanding what the right choice is. However, this lesson is often learned by doing the wrong thing and regretting it later.

A friend of mine, Billy, coached an inner-city junior wrestling club. It was common for youngsters to be brought to the club by police, social services or desperate parents seeking a sporting solution to a behavioural problem. These young people very often did not do the right thing and made bad choices. Lack of discipline and self-control caused them to fail repeatedly. Wrestling is a sport where you are on your own in the arena, and discipline and self-control are essential elements. Billy would start by building character, teaching these youngsters how to do the right thing and develop good habits. When they arrived in the gym for training, Billy insisted they earned the right to participate by demonstrating the beginnings of self-discipline. The young wrestlers had to start each evening by going over to Billy and wishing him good evening, shaking his hand and showing him a bottle full of water clearly labelled with their name. If they completed these actions to Billy's satisfaction, they were allowed to join the other coaches and wrestlers on the mats, but if they did not, Billy refused to allow them to participate.

Billy understood that self-discipline opens the door to all other areas of development. By making these young wrestlers go through this start-of-the-evening procedure, Billy was teaching them to take responsibility for their preparation and actions, to show a commitment to learning, to understand how to earn the respect of other people and have the reward of being granted the rights that go along with that. Billy used this tough-love coaching approach to help these young people grow into responsible adults despite the drawback of a difficult environment. Some of them have now become coaches themselves.

When the chairman of a European football club asked me why the young players coming through from the youth academy were not mentally strong enough to survive in the senior first-team environment, I knew the club should first change their approach to youth recruitment. They had made the mistake of stressing the entitlements (financial support, accommodation, education and other benefits) available to the players and families rather than the responsibilities required from a young footballer aiming for a professional career. This led to misconceptions about what behaviours were acceptable from young players and led to poor standards on and off the training pitches, for instance being late, wearing the wrong kit, avoiding jobs and making excuses. Too many entitlements get in the way of developing resilience and mental toughness. The policy was reversed, and responsibilities were placed before rights – 'if you carry out your responsibilities you'll receive the appropriate benefits'.

To follow up and reinforce this policy, the coaches at each age level in the academy were asked to determine, agree and implement a small number of age-appropriate responsibilities for their players. These non-negotiable behaviours gave players an increasing level of responsibility alongside their football development as they moved up through the academy system. The messages that all players were receiving were:

- Be where you are supposed to be, when you are supposed to be there.
- Do what you are supposed to do, when you are supposed to do it.
- Do what you say you are going to do.
- Do it for yourself and to help the team.
- Be responsible for your job – players who can be trusted get rewarded.
- Be accountable – accept feedback.

Slowly, like the young wrestlers, the football academy players began to take more responsibility for their behaviour and accepted accountability when they failed. Under the right conditions, young players learn quickly. Behaviour, good habits and character improved as they took pride in doing the right things repeatedly. This transferred into performance on the field, and the club developed more disciplined players with higher levels of self-control. There were many talented young players at the club, but often the talent had been unfulfilled under pressure because of a lack of character and the tendency to make the wrong choices. As this new system progressed we saw players transferring to the senior teams with the benefit of both talent and character. It was pleasing to see their success.

It is not always easy to do the right thing repeatedly and habitually. It is a key step towards a successful life, though many people make the mistake of believing this only applies to the big issues. What Billy's story and the football academy approach teaches us is that if we can demonstrate these standards consistently in the small, day-to-day elements of our lives we will develop the habits that help us be successful and resolute in the situations that really matter. Such an approach is fundamental to the philosophy of military organizations. When in critical situations, following guidelines learned and practised in training can help to avert imminent danger and save lives.

In most situations, people know what the right thing to do is. If they continue to make the wrong choices, they must work out what gets in their way of making a different choice. From personal experience, I have occasionally not done the right thing (usually when tired, over-emotional or simply not thinking through the likely consequences) and suffered with guilt the next day. The words attributed to Abraham Lincoln – 'When I do good, I feel good. When I do bad, I feel bad. That's my religion' – are so true. How often do we drift through the day and then at night feel we have achieved nothing? What if we resolve to do the right thing more often, to become a more accountable person and thus feel good when we go to bed?

'WHAT IF WE RESOLVE TO DO THE RIGHT THING MORE OFTEN?'

PUT IT INTO ACTION

- Before acting, pause and ask yourself, 'What is the right thing to do?'
- Avoid hasty decisions when off-balance physically or mentally.
- If in doubt, give yourself a 'time-out'.
- Accept responsibility when you get things wrong.
- Learn to avoid making the same mistakes again.

LESSON 18:

CONTROL THE CONTROLLABLES - PLAY TO YOUR STRENGTHS

Becoming a performance psychologist changed my life, professionally and personally. I have already confessed that sometimes I fell captive to my emotions and took unwise decisions and actions. Performance psychology taught me that in the emotional aftermath of difficult situations my clouded thinking had been dominated by the 'uncontrollables', for example, 'What will other people think?', 'Will I get the job?' These were things in such situations that I had no power over. One day, I heard a great saying: 'You cannot always control the situation you find yourself in, but you can always control your response.' The answer lies in putting the uncontrollables to one side and focusing on thinking through the things that you can control, leading to a more rational response. Now, when faced by the 'red mist' that comes when things go wrong, I ask myself, 'What can I do about this?' and begin to deal with the situation by thinking through my options rather than have an over-emotional reaction.

I spotted Jake as someone who has learned the lesson of dealing with, and not reacting to, challenging situations.

Twenty basketball players had gathered to try out for the ten spots available for the team to contest the European Championships. Right from the start, Jake's attitude stood out, though it was clear he wasn't as technically talented as many of the other players. Each evening, I listened as the coaches focused on talent and missed the potential of Jake's contribution. When they ranked the players on talent, I could not disagree with Jake's ranking of between fifteenth and twentieth in the group. So I produced another ranking list based on attitude and teamship with Jake ranked number one. The coaches then took a closer look at him and saw the attitude of a winner:

- always early for practice
- always smart and well prepared
- a 'can do' attitude
- enthusiastic/high-energy
- enjoys learning
- undeterred by mistakes
- selfless and a team player
- accepts feedback
- takes responsibility
- supports teammates
- a pleasure to work with

The coaches accepted that attitude and character would be as important as talent in the European arena and selected Jake. In a successful tournament, Jake was the standout player both on and off the court. Time and time again he proved he could be trusted.

The environment of a sporting event is often quite chaotic. It becomes very important that the athlete doesn't become distracted but rather focuses on what they can control and plays to their strengths. However, it is not always easy for younger athletes to avoid the distractions of the 'sideshow', and their focus can be overcome by what they cannot control. Michael, a seventeen-year-old basketball player, was described by his coach as the best talent he had ever worked with, and when Michael came to the senior team, great things were expected from him. Unfortunately, his performance disintegrated in the harsh spotlight of the main arena. Michael was so sensitive to the importance of the game and the judgement of his teammates, the opponents, spectators and the media that he could not focus on his own performance. Our conversations centred on helping him remove the fear of the judgement of others, learning to emotionally detach and accept the mantra 'it is what it is'.

To help illustrate the kind of mental strength Michael needed to develop I used the story of the Olympic swimmer Michael Phelps, who broke his wrist while training for the 2008 Olympics in Beijing. In order to stay in control of the situation he ignored the distraction of what he couldn't control and continued training by only working on his legs while his wrist healed. He went on to win eight gold medals. Michael, the young basketball player, did improve but unfortunately not enough to become the player his coach had once anticipated.

Everyone has strengths and weaknesses, but the winners work on their weaknesses while maximizing their strengths. There were aspects of the game that Jake could not perform as well as his teammates on the basketball court; however, there were skills within his control that he brought in abundance to the benefit of the team's performance. Focusing on weaknesses that you cannot control can easily become an excuse for not performing at your best. Your attitude is your responsibility and your choice. Harvard University recognized this in recent years by changing their admissions policy for undergraduate courses to focus on talent 50 per cent and character and attitude 50 per cent. Similarly, when I was a college lecturer, interviewing for admission to degree-level courses, I had three key questions for prospective students that helped reveal their attitude and character:

1. Who are you?
2. Who do you want to be?
3. Tell us three things that you have achieved that you are proud of that were not compulsory.

Characteristic of successful people in sport and life is that they are both effective and efficient. The efficiency comes from being able to separate the controllables – 'I should be able to do something about this' – from the

'EVERYONE HAS STRENGTHS AND WEAKNESSES, BUT THE WINNERS WORK ON THEIR WEAKNESSES WHILE MAXIMIZING THEIR STRENGTHS' uncontrollables – 'I cannot affect these things.' The effectiveness is generated by maximizing their knowledge, experience, time and energy on the things that significantly improve the chances of being successful. As Jake's list of characteristics shows, these can be simple, doable actions that, with focus and effort, may be undertaken easily. Both Jake and Michael Phelps demonstrated that the one thing that everyone can control is the amount of hard work they are willing to invest, plus an unwillingness to dwell on uncontrollable factors. This mindset ensures they stay emotionally in control. Our young basketball player Michael, however, was beset with anxieties about things he could not do anything about, and his performance was limited by the resultant lack of emotional control.

PUT IT INTO ACTION

Imagine your situation is going for a new job or a trial with a sports team:
- List what are the key factors for success.
- Separate out the things you can't control and 'park' them.
- Bring your strengths to bear on the things you can impact.
- If you fail because of uncontrollables, accept that 'that's life' and move on – you did your best!

LESSON 19:

MODEL YOUR BEHAVIOUR – ACT LIKE YOUR HERO

When Steve McClaren left Manchester United to join Middlesbrough FC as manager, he asked me to move with him as assistant manager. Our opening game was at home. We were beaten 0–4. I watched as Steve had to contend with his own disappointment, the reaction of the fans and the depression of his players and staff. As though that wasn't enough, Steve then had to face the national press. I could feel his anxiety as we walked towards the media room. Casually, I asked how he thought Alex Ferguson, the manager at Manchester United, would deal with this. Steve stopped and described how Alex would remain strong, positive and dominate the room. I suggested that he should be Alex for the next fifteen minutes. Steve modelled his behaviour on our former boss and dealt with a challenging situation very well, while also learning a good lesson for the future.

Much of our behaviour is based on observing, imitating and modelling ourselves on the behaviour of those people who are, or who have been, significant in our lives. I could not personally model the behaviour that would help Steve, nor could it be described effectively and swiftly in words. However, a meaningful symbolic image that Steve would appreciate offered a good chance of how best he could deal with the situation. The image of a great role model in a particular situation can have a powerful impact.

The introduction of an influential role figure can also be a very significant source of informal modelling. At one particular football club where I was working, the squad contained a number of players towards the end of their careers who demonstrated poor habits and a lack of professionalism. Our concern was the effect on the talented group of young players who had just come into the squad. However, this was taken care of for us by the arrival of a well-chosen senior player as a new signing. From day one, this player, chosen for his character as well as his talent, quietly set a new standard of professionalism – arriving early, looking smart and ready to go and always giving maximum focus and effort. The young players simply took one look at the two choices on offer, modelled themselves on the new signing, and standards improved. This group was then the catalyst for one of the club's most successful periods.

Finding a significant role model was again useful when helping a top professional goalkeeper, Andy, who had a problem in coming out from his goal and claiming balls crossed from wide positions. He was extremely talented, though this one serious flaw got him in trouble with the manager. My initial thoughts were based around answering the question 'Can't do or won't do?' I quickly rejected 'can't do' – Andy was tall and athletic with great ball skills – so I focused on a mindset problem that was getting in the way of his performance.

When I raised this issue with Andy, an intelligent and thoughtful individual, he explained that coming out to deal with crosses was risky, and he did not want to let the team down by making a significant mistake. I asked him why the manager would ask him to do such a risky thing. After some thought, his reply showed that he understood the important messages that a confident approach to dealing with crosses would send to both the opposition and his own team. Having got him to accept there was a need for change, the next step was to find a motivation that would overcome his mental block.

His favourite goalkeeper was Peter Schmeichel, so the next day we prepared a ten-minute film compilation of Peter coming out of his goal to claim crosses. I suggested to Andy that he should try to model his behaviour on Schmeichel. 'Just be Peter,' I urged him. Gradually, through training sessions and games, he began to reproduce the desired reaction to crosses with increasing confidence. The reward was continued selection and positive feedback from his manager and the team. Andy integrated this modelled behaviour into his considerable range of skills, and it became recognized as a fundamental strength of his goalkeeping career.

'KEEP ASKING
YOURSELF WHAT YOUR
"HERO" WOULD DO
AND THEN FIND THE
COURAGE TO DO IT'

In seeking to improve ourselves, we are likely to be challenged to produce behaviour that we're not comfortable with. Such situations are key moments to learn. The easy option is to give in, 'it's too difficult'. However, if we can bring to mind a successful and personally significant role model with the necessary skills, we can observe and then imitate their behaviour until it becomes natural to us. Just like Andy asking himself what Peter would do, simply keep asking yourself what your 'hero' would do and then find the courage to do it. The rewards will make it very worthwhile.

PUT IT INTO ACTION

- Study the people who are excellent at a goal you are aiming to achieve.
- Select a role model and in a given situation ask yourself, 'What would they do?'
- If your actions fall short, check whether your issue is that you 'can't do' or 'won't do'. If you 'can't do', the action you need is to practise more or continue learning. If you 'won't do', the action you then need is to work on changing your thinking.

LESSON 20:

KEEP A JOURNAL – RELEASE YOUR FEARS AND MOVE ON

I am now at the stage in my career where many of the players I helped some years ago are now coaches and managers themselves. One such football manager, Bruno, invited me to work with his team. As he introduced me to the team in our first meeting, he produced a kit bag, almost too heavy for him to lift, full of his hand-written journals. Writing personal events into a journal was a practice he had begun when I helped him as a young player newly arrived in England. He showed the team to illustrate how he had valued this process so much that he had maintained his journal-writing activity through-out his long career.

Bruno was a polite and quite shy young man at our first meeting many years ago. In the space of a few days, he had gone from living in the familiar surroundings of home, family and friends, being a talented player in his local club and a new member of his national team, to being recruited into a club in the English Premier League. His anxiety began when he walked into the dressing room and found himself in the company of all his footballing heroes. He felt like an imposter and convinced himself that he couldn't possibly match the level of expertise in the room. Every day had become a battle for him as this growing anxiety began to affect his attitude and performance.

He had a negative train of thought running in his head – 'I'm not as good as the rest of the team, I don't belong here. I can't become a great player' – that he ruminated on continually. He believed these thoughts, and that knocked his confidence and thus drained his energy. When I checked with the club coaches, they said they were still convinced that Bruno could become a truly great player, though they recognized he was having anxiety issues. It was clear the problem was Bruno's alone; his coaches believed in him, but he found personal evidence to support his negative thoughts. He would have to face and win a personal battle to find the positivity needed to overcome his anxiety.

We began our work together by discussing the idea that everything provides an opportunity to learn and grow, and he could emerge from this mental struggle as a stronger and better player. To help him make sense of the conversation in his head, I suggested he should keep a journal. The very act of transferring thoughts to paper can relieve the clutter in the mind, help get thoughts in order and bring a sense of relief. Bruno agreed that he would build up this written examination of his mind by answering four questions in his journal, maybe not every day, though a regular discipline would be a benefit. First, he would note down what went wrong that day, followed by how he could change it. Then he would write about what went well that day, and finally how he could improve. This became an evening exercise to recall the lows and highs of the day.

Each time we met, we would check his journal, and gradually over time, as our sessions progressed, Bruno began to distinguish reality from his perceptions as we challenged the evidence. Initially, he shared his feelings about missing a chance to score in practice and how it undermined his confidence for the rest of the training session. This was a good basis to begin to shift his thinking away from the very negative. Then he shared the actions he would take to bring about change for his perceived negative issues. For instance, his response to missing a chance to score was that he would learn to 'park' this negativity and get stronger not weaker. I reminded him that great strikers only average about one goal in every five attempts but don't let those stats affect their confidence. Slowly, he was beginning to exert more control over his mind. Next, we looked at his assessment of 'what went well today?' Bruno wrote that he had worked hard to lose his defender and get in a position to score and, although he missed, he had taken responsibility.

People are more sensitive and vulnerable to negative feelings than positive ones, and a negative frame of mind can result in blinding us to progress. We spend so much time looking at what went wrong that we forget to look at what went right. In that sense, the humility that was part of Bruno's nature was also getting in his way.

It was vital for Bruno to stop blocking out the good parts of his performance and acknowledge what the coaches and his teammates could clearly see: that he was a very good player. To facilitate this shift in his thinking we agreed to invite one of the assistant coaches to one of our sessions to share his views on Bruno's ability and performance. This acted as a tremendous boost to his confidence, as the coach emphasized Bruno's good qualities and that he was an important part of the team's future. In addition, from then on, that coach took a real interest in Bruno's progress and became a belief partner. Extra positive reinforcement came when we reviewed the film clips I'd asked the club's video analyst to prepare showing the assists and attacking moves Bruno had made in the previous week's games.

Over the weeks, we explored the last entry included in his evening journal entries, his ideas on 'How can I get better?' Bruno, by now taking more responsibility for his situation, decided he would work harder on shooting techniques and remaining calm when chances occurred.

It was very rewarding to see Bruno take more control of his thinking and become a more confident and assertive person and player as the season progressed. His belief in the value of keeping a journal was demonstrated many years later by his producing these historic diaries in front of his own team when I visited.

'WE SPEND SO MUCH TIME LOOKING AT WHAT WENT WRONG THAT WE FORGET TO LOOK AT WHAT WENT RIGHT'

PUT IT INTO ACTION

In times of anxiety, we might all benefit from writing our thoughts down and decluttering the mind. If you feel this might work for you, follow the steps that Bruno took:

1. What went wrong today?
2. How can I change that?
3. What went well today?
4. How can I get better?

Remember that an important ingredient in the process is finding a friend or mentor who can help you challenge the evidence and reinforce what you do well. Then for you, in the same way as for Bruno, keeping a journal can become a life-changing and life-expanding activity.

SOME FINAL THOUGHTS

I could not have written a book like this if it were not for a stream of feedback received from former clients and students. At the time I helped them, most were so busy establishing their performance careers that many forgot to say thank you. Later in their lives, and with the time and wisdom that promotes reflection, many contacted me to make amends. However, the interesting thing is, while they mentioned their sporting progress, they talked far more of how our work together had made them a better person. It is almost inevitable that when you work closely with someone on solving a performance problem the conversation takes a personal turn. What is especially remembered is the teaching of these five keys to happiness and flourishing in today's world:

Purpose: having something to get up for in the morning.
People: being surrounded by loving relationships.
Place: living in a place that makes you happy.
Health: being healthy in all senses.

Financial security: not worrying about money now
   or for the future.

It has always been my belief that it is not what you achieve from sport that matters most, it is who you become, and the significance of the feedback I have received has encouraged me to share such stories with you, not necessarily for what you could get from life but for who you might become.

The other comment former clients make from the perspective of time and distance is of how much more fulfilling life became when they stopped getting in their own way, stopped feeling helpless and actively started to rewrite their story by taking control of the events of their life. I do hope that sharing my experiences might encourage you to do the same.

The dominant theme woven through this book is that the struggle for psychological health and well-being is one of you versus you – the strong you versus the weak you. The stories emphasize the power of seeking help and not trying to battle life on your own. In some way or form all my athletes and coaches have found the courage to say, 'I was wrong,' 'I am sorry,' 'I don't know,' or 'I need help.' For some of those individuals the act of sharing with a mentor or thinking partner unlocked the key to changing their story and a much more successful career – and life.

This simple book of stories encourages you to review

your own life story and reminds you that your life can begin to change the moment you accept responsibility for your own mindset, consequent thinking and behaviour. If you are not leading the life you want, there are a number of ways, illustrated in each lesson, that you can regain control. The key questions to answer are, 'What do I want?' and 'How much do I want it?' Change is not easy, but if you can overcome any fears and doubts and summon up the willpower to take responsibility and strengthen your mindset, you can reshape the course of your life.

I wish you well in Changing Your Story!

Bill

MANAGE YOUR PROGRESS - CHECKLISTS TO HELP

Everyone benefits from reminders, so here are some checklists to stimulate thinking and help your progress.

CHECKLIST 1: KNOW YOURSELF

This exercise helps you build a picture of yourself now and guides you towards creating a vision statement of who you want to be. A vision statement should provide direction and be imaginative, inspirational, clearly stated, focused, future-oriented and promote a standard of excellence for yourself.

To create your vision statement, answer the following questions:

1. My favourite teacher / coach was . . .
   What I loved and appreciated about them was . . .

2. Something I am proud of is when . . .
   I was successful then because . . .

3. My greatest strengths are . . .
   The strengths I want to develop are . . .

4. The way I want to live is . . .
   I want to be remembered for . . .

5. I am at my best when . . .

6. I am deeply passionate about . . .

7. I love doing what I do because . . .

8. What is really important in my life is . . .
   What I want to accomplish is . . .

Now pick out the key words that are important to you and put them all together to create your personal vision statement (no more than five sentences).

CHECKLIST 2: BELIEVE IN YOURSELF

Your performance will always mirror your self-belief, so building belief in yourself is key to the process of Changing Your Story. This checklist serves as a reminder of the building blocks of belief. Refer to it regularly.

- Do not impose personal limits – surprise yourself.

- Belief is a choice – be brave and back yourself.

- Belief is motivated by evidence – remember your history of successes.

- Earn your belief through preparation and hard work.

- Take pride even in small successes.

- Belief relies on positive self-talk – be your own cheerleader.

- Belief is fuelled (or not) by the people in your life – choose friends who challenge you to be better.

- Believe in others and they will believe in you.

- Belief is always tested by setbacks – do not waver!

- The only failure is giving up – never give in!

CHECKLIST 3: CHOOSING TO BE POSITIVE

Our mood, morale and general state of happiness depends on our interpretation of the situations we face. Choosing to be positive – 'I can with effort deal with this' – is the basis of successful coping. This checklist is designed for you to read and help take your mindset into that positive state, so read it regularly and especially when you recognize the onset of negative thinking.

- I believe in myself.

- I can deal with most things.

- I always talk myself up.

- I come to compete every day.

- I will not surrender to giving up.

- I never turn against myself in the tough times.

- I focus on my strengths and contain my weaknesses.

- I take setbacks as learning opportunities.

- I will be a good team member.

- I never blame or make excuses and accept responsibility for my actions.

- I will not come second best to myself.

CHECKLIST 4: FIGHTER OR VICTIM MENTALITY?

This book refers a number of times to the choice facing everyone when challenged – fighter or victim mentality. You are encouraged to adopt a fighter mentality, but it is recognized that we all occasionally find ourselves thinking like victims. The following checklist acts as a guide to assess your ongoing mental state.

Fighter Mentality	*Victim Mentality*
Takes responsibility	Always seeking excuses
Needs to achieve	Comfortable with losing
Stays in control	Gives up control easily
Enjoys the challenge	Endures the challenge
Stays positive	Hides under pressure
Loves being coached	Can't take criticism
Focuses on strengths	Dominated by weaknesses
Deals with 'uncomfortable'	Returns to 'comfort zone'
Seeks friends who challenge	Chooses 'victim' friends
Loves the game	Loves the sideshow

CHECKLIST 5: COMMITTING TO A CHAMPION MINDSET

Champions are determined by their talent and their mindset. There are many examples in this book of the mindset of champions in action. This checklist indicates the way a champion's mindset is developed. Can you learn from this?

- Find your passion every day.

- Set short, medium and longer-term goals.

- Take responsibility – be accountable.

- Commit to the plan every day – be willing to work hard.

- Build a support group – people who believe in you.

- Grow your talent – learn every day.

- Only focus on what you can control.

- Deal with setbacks – don't react emotionally.

- Know when/how to relax and recover.

- Make good lifestyle choices 24/7/365.

- Never give in – keep seeing the possibilities.

- Always remember – the opponent is YOU!

CHECKLIST 6: TEN STEPS TO SELF-MANAGEMENT

This checklist is to help you stop getting in your own way and instead build a daily winning mindset. Check in with it as often as you can so place it where you can't miss it; for example, on the bathroom mirror or fridge door. You can evaluate your day by rechecking in the evening.

1. Take responsibility for your day – no excuses.
2. Set out to achieve at least three targets.
3. Think positively – 'Today will be a good day.'
4. Ignore what you can't control.
5. Be assertive – decide to be a fighter, not a victim.
6. Manage your time and energy – be efficient.
7. Be the example – early, prepared and enthusiastic.
8. Love the challenge – 'Today is my chance to shine.'
9. Learn something new every day.
10. Be a leader – make the people around you better.

Acknowledgements

This book would never have taken shape without the coaches and athletes who found the courage to seek my help and say 'I have a problem, I need help . . .'. Your stories will now help others to face their fears.

There is always a team behind the team and this project would not have been possible for me without the help of a very talented support group. For their 'sense reading', valuable feedback and encouragement, I owe thanks to Hayley Beswick and Diane Patterson.

It was my editor at Penguin, Emily Robertson, who proposed this book after being at one of my presentations. From the very start Emily, ably assisted by Susannah Bennett, has been a believer, providing a stream of helpful suggestions and prompting me forward when I wavered. Thank you!

A final but special thanks to my wife, Val, who acts as my personal truth-teller and brought discipline and professionalism to the process, especially during the tough stages of bringing it to completion.

I make no comment on the fact I am surrounded by lovely and talented women.